W9-CER-061

dead
and
buried

the horrible history of bodysnatching

dead and buried

the horrible history of bodysnatching

?

NORMAN ADAMS

BELL PUBLISHING COMPANY
NEW YORK

Copyright © MCMLXXII by Norman Adams
Library of Congress Catalog Card Number: 74-75919
All rights reserved.
This edition is published by Bell Publishing Co., Inc.
a division of Crown Publishers, Inc.
by arrangement with Impulse Publications, Ltd.
a b c d e f g h
Manufactured in the United States of America

Contents

142264

Illustrations

The author and publishers are indebted to the following for their assistance with the illustration of this book:

Professor G. J. Romanes, Dept. of Anatomy, Edinburgh University Medical School

Mr. J. W. Cockburn, City Librarian and Curator, Edinburgh Corporation Libraries and Museums Dept.

Mr. Charles Bernan, United Artists Ltd.

The Mary Evans Picture Library

Ken Lennox and J. Geddes Wood

And as for my feet, the little feet,
You used to call so pretty,
There's one, I know, in Bedford Row,
The t'others in the city.

THOMAS HOOD 1799-1845

The Lady Vanishes

—

On a dreary February day in 1809, the body of a naked woman was washed up on the rocks at the Bay of Nigg, less than two miles down the coast from Aberdeen. The grim discovery of a drowned and decomposed corpse in these exposed waters is not uncommon; for the deep claims its share of life over the years. The North Sea gives up its dead after a struggle, but the discovery of the body of Mrs Janet Spark caused a great stir in the parish of Nigg for a different reason.

Six weeks earlier she had been buried in the small, picturesque graveyard at St Fittick's Kirk, a few hundred yards up the brae from the rocky bite of the Bay of Nigg.

The macabre meanderings of the late Mrs Spark, which horrified and revolted the simple God-fearing farmers and fisherfolk in what was then a remote corner of Kincardineshire presents a grim Scottish introduction to three incredible decades in British social history. The age of the body-snatchers. For the unfortunate Mrs Spark had been lifted from her grave at St Fittick's by resurrectionists only a few hours after her funeral, and only a strange quirk of fate prevented her aged body from becoming a "subject" for the anatomy class at the Marischal College in Aberdeen.

From Land's End to John o' Groats, people lived and died in terror of the body-snatchers, for the old saying you are worth more dead than alive was certainly true then of the poor, and very dead, parishioners throughout the country. Even the rich, in the beginning, fell easy prey until their money found a way to cheat the resurrectionists and the anatomist's knife, for a little while.

It was the era of the Edinburgh monsters, Burke and Hare, and their London imitators, Bishop and Williams, the 'Corpse-King' Ben Crouch, and a legion of eager medical students, who risked life and limb to swoop on newly-dug graves to further the cause of medical science. There were cases where mourners followed empty coffins to the cemeteries, because the corpses were stolen before burial; the dead were hawked around medical schools and sold to the highest bidder and men, women and children were deliberately murdered to keep up the supply for medical students.

But as one modern Scots doctor wrote: "We must draw the line of distinction between them (the anatomists and their students) and the ghouls who scraped a precarious livelihood from the foulest trade in human history." He pointed out that the students' one desire was to advance the cause of science, while the other crowd were only interested in furthering their own gain. They robbed corpses of their jewellery, their teeth, and even the fat from their bodies found a market.

The stark terror of innocent Scots in those distant days is reflected by a past Aberdeen historian William Buchanan, who recalled in 1870: "If any person went from home longer than usual, they were sure to have been 'Burked'. The hair-breadth escapes from sticking-plasters, and being pursued by doctors, that were retailed each morning were truly wonderful, and timid people were afraid to go out after dark."

To the nineteenth-century Glaswegian the dark, evil-smelling wynds off the Trongate harboured a host of body-snatchers, poised with chloroform pad and sack, ready for the unsuspecting. Anxious parents warned their children to keep clear of the Old Wynd, which had a grim reputation, although, as far as is known, no pedestrian was actually 'Burked'. For many, many years after the resurrectionist era young and old who passed the wynd would clap a hand over their mouths to prevent the chloroform from taking effect, even if they did not know the reason why they did so. The 'Burkers' were blamed for snatching a Forfar gent after he had vanished on a drinking spree. Suspicion fell on his cronies, and their lives were made intolerable until their missing friend's body turned up in a ditch after the winter snow melted.

To talk of romance in a graveyard in the dead of night may seem out of place. But there is no doubt the medical students faced grave risks to enrich their knowledge of life. Apart from running the risk of breaking the law and facing heavy fines, they could ill afford, or, even worse, a stiff jail sentence, they had to run the gauntlet of the watchers of the dead; the relatives who mounted a nightly guard over the graves of their dear departed, and heaven help the resurrectionist who fell into their clutches! Captive body-snatchers were tossed into rivers, whipped and kicked and there was an instance when a young Scots doctor was so terribly beaten he never fully recovered.

Walk into any graveyard today and the evidence of those terrible yet exciting days, lies at your feet. The table-topped grave stones and iron grilled mort-safes which were used to baulk the work of the 'sack-'em-up men'. These curious devices served their purpose, but only for a short time, until the body-snatchers found a way to overcome them. As the raids intensified in town and country, watch-houses and look-out towers were built; the dead were enclosed in iron coffins or sealed in vaults, but there were always corpses available, if the price was right.

In 1828, Sir Astley Cooper, President of the Royal College of Surgeons in London, boasted to a Select Committee set up to investigate the manner of obtaining subjects for the schools of anatomy: "There is no person, let his situation in life be what it may, who, if I were disposed to dissect, I could not obtain."

Sir Astley was dubbed, 'The King of the Resurrectionists'. He was their self-appointed patron and protector. He enjoyed practical jokes, and, of course, had a passion for dissection. When he was not dissecting a body at St Thomas's Hospital or at Guy's Hospital just across the road, he was hard at work in his private anatomical theatre in his home in St Mary Axe, London. He would dissect anything from a dog to an elephant, which he did, in 1801. The elephant had died at the menagerie in the Tower of London, and its mammoth carcase was dragged through narrow streets to his yard.

Sir Astley had a huge army of body-snatchers at his disposal and he paid them vast sums to keep the tables in his medical schools well stocked. One of his agents claimed he paid a top London body-snatcher £72 for six bodies, and later the same evening he saw the same man receive a further £72 for six more corpses, freshly-plucked from the grave. Dr Robert Knox, the Edinburgh anatomist who was ruined because of his dealings with Burke and Hare, who were not resurrectionists, paid out an estimated £700 to £800 in one year to keep his students happy.

But not every anatomist could afford to pay such large sums to secure bodies. When this happened, particularly in Scotland, it was left to the students themselves to go out in search of 'subjects'. And in some cases teacher went too. Dr Andrew Moir, founder of the Aberdeen school of anatomy, regularly went foraging for specimens with members of his class.

The eminent Edinburgh surgeon, Robert Liston, was always willing to go hunting for bodies, but just for the hell of it. He was not short of cash. He took part in lightning raids on cemeteries in the fishing villages of Fife across the Firth of Forth, and was accompanied on one particularly legendary swoop by Ben Crouch, who had come north of the border when things became too hot for him in London.

Body-snatching became big business and earned huge fortunes for the professionals. Stolen corpses were illegally imported from Ireland and France, while British boats plied between London and several Scottish ports with their ghastly cargo. Burke and Hare had planned to go into the import business in Glasgow before they became careless and were caught.

Then, in 1832, after the multiple murders in Edinburgh and London, and the burning of Andrew Moir's 'Burking Hoose' in Aberdeen, the Government took dramatic steps which ended the gruesome trade. The Anatomy Act introduced by Henry Warburton provided a legal supply of bodies to the country's anatomical schools. The body-snatching age was over.

But in North-east Scotland in the winter of 1808 it was just beginning. There had been several raids on cemeteries in the area since the turn of the century, but none as unusual as Mrs Spark's sudden disappearance from her resting place at Nigg. Mrs Spark's funeral took place three days before Christmas Day. She was the widow of an Aberdeen shipmaster and the step-mother of Thomas Spark, for many years the treasurer of Aberdeen Royal Infirmary. She was 90 years old when she died in her home in the Shiprow, and on the day of her funeral the cortege was conveyed across the River Dee to Torry by ferry boat.

As the mourners made their way over the steep hill to the kirkyard and the bay beyond, they paid little attention to two young men who had accompanied them on the boat journey. The resurrectionists relied heavily on their fifth column to keep them in touch with the dates and times of burials. Undertakers were bribed to fit weak fastenings to the coffins and sometimes gravediggers were paid to pinpoint fresh graves, or even remove the bodies by themselves.

The two strangers were medical students, but it was not until the following morning that their presence outside the kirkyard gates was recalled. By then it was too late. It was believed that the body-snatchers were disturbed by the barking and approach of the parish minister's dog from the nearby manse. They partly filled the grave, but carelessly left behind a spade with a vital clue: the name, 'Rae' carved on the handle.

The coffin had been crudely opened. Broken pieces were scattered around the open grave, tatters of a shroud and traces of blood were found on the coffin lid. There was no sign of poor Mrs Spark. When the kirk session met at their weekly meeting on Christmas Day the minister informed them of the horrific details of the robbery. As they gathered in his manse to hear the awful story, the friends and relatives of Mrs Spark, formerly Janet Young, were searching for her missing corpse. In the kirk's register of discipline it is recorded that "the session resolved to await a little the event of their endeavours to find out this daring and alarming thing, which might have very bad consequences on the minds of the people, and to do everything in their power to prevent such conduct".

In the following weeks nothing was recorded of the search for missing Mrs Spark, but when the session met on February 12, 1809, the mystery had been solved. Mrs Spark had been found, and was safely back in her grave. What had happened to her body after the 'snatch' the previous December reads like a black comedy. The students who dug up her body had decided not to risk ferrying the corpse back to the city that same night and had therefore buried it in a bank of sand at the north end of the Bay of Nigg, with the intention of returning to collect it the following day. But because of the hue and cry throughout the Nigg parish, and Aberdeen, the students stayed well clear of the spot. Then, something completely unforeseen took place. A great storm swept the North-east and the coast was pounded by high seas. The waves crashed down on the shore at the Bay of Nigg and when they retreated they carried off Mrs Spark. Her corpse bobbed and floated in the bay until the following February when it was spotted on the south side.

The minister at Nigg informed his elders at the February meeting that "the person principally concerned in taking up the body was found to be a forward, impudent, not well behaved young man, a student in physic, who had been obliged to flee from the country".

The name of the offending student was not recorded at the meeting, but it does not require a great piece of detective work to know that his name was Rae. The spade he left behind in the kirkyard belonged to his father. And from further statements in the kirk records it seems obvious his father had to pay a large amount of compensation to the dead woman's family to prevent a scandal. The minister put it thus: "So much trouble and expense to his father, so much vexation to the woman's relatives, and such resentment of the world has taken place, with fear of the consequences of such conduct that no apprehension was entertained of anything like it again being attempted."

This particular entry ends on an optimistic note: "The minister had publicly intimated the circumstances of the whole, with the great danger to any who should try such a thing, which seemed to quiet the public mind. The session judged nothing further proper to be now done." But the little kirkyard, abandoned by its congregation in 1829, and today a picturesque ruin, became a fruitful source of supply for the Aberdeen resurrectionists. But unlike those responsible for stealing Mrs Spark's body, they obeyed the first rule of the bodysnatchers' code: always remember to replace the turf. Even so, in 1816, the minister and his elders felt confident that nothing of the sort had been repeated since the Spark scandal, even although the congregation had other views.

Each week the St Fittick's session met to discuss the news and gossip of the parish and to hand out punishment and fines to wrongdoers, or to fix fees for grave-digging, and so on. Sometimes they would have a particularly world-shattering item on their agenda. Such as warning those members of their flock who dared violate the Sabbath by hunting for seagulls' eggs on the towering cliffs at Cove; or endorse Aberdeen Presbytery's edict which forbade bathing or boating on a Sunday. They also dealt with the sinners and there were numerous cases where parishioners had committed the 'sin of antenuptial fornication'.

But in April 1816 the session admitted that "there had been an apprehension among the people of the parish, that bodies of the dead, buried in the churchyard might be taken up for dissection by students of medicine, which excited uneasiness, and occasional trouble and expense in watching the graves upon an internment". It had been agreed to quell such fears by providing the crudest type of mort-safe, a huge, dressed granite stone. This stone, which was about the same length as a coffin, would be lowered over the coffin in the grave before burial. It was then removed some weeks later when it was thought the body would be of no use to the anatomists. The Nigg stone was gifted to the kirk by Superintendent Gibb of Aberdeen Harbour Works, and it cost 2s 6d to transport the heavy load by cart from the ferry landing stage to the churchyard.

The kirk session "thought that there was no reason to apprehend" such a thing as body-snatching at their kirk in the future, but they were whistling in the dark. For at this period body-snatching was the rage, with the peace of graveyards shattered by gunshots, and the sound of horse-drawn gigs and carts trundling through deserted streets and lanes after dark. Kirkyards within a certain radius of a city with a medical school were a certain target. Before long, St Fittick's, like other churches in the neighbourhood, provided its own watch-house, where relatives kept guard for nights on end, warmed from the chill night air by a roaring fire or a wee dram or two.

But those long, weary vigils were sometimes fruitless tasks, for the body-snatchers sometimes struck in daylight before the watchers came on duty. Or the resurrectionists would wait until the grey light of dawn when the guards were fast asleep, or too drunk to care.

St Fittick's Churchyard was certainly not impregnable, and

at least two other unknown corpses almost shared the same fate as Mrs Spark. They too were abandoned by the medical students, who did not return to claim the bodies. This particular mystery came to light in 1874 when the Dee was being diverted into its present channel.

On trenching the garden behind Jessie Petrie's old inn at the bottom of Ferry Road, Old Torry, two skeletons were found. Villagers believed the body-snatchers had hidden the bodies behind the inn while they had gone inside for a well-deserved refreshment. But someone had disturbed them and they had obviously quit the place in a great hurry. The ferry boat had plied between Footdee's Harbour Blockhouse on the north side of the Dee and Old Torry since before 1648.

The inn was a popular howf of the ferry passengers. One particularly cold night in February 1829, two strangers sat themselves down at the roaring fire and ordered drink. They told the landlord's wife they had crossed from Aberdeen and their destination was Altens, a few miles down the Kincardineshire coast, to buy cattle. As they left the inn one of them bought a bottle of whisky. He rubbed his hands, remarked on the weather, and suggested he and his companion should call with a dram on the watchmen in St Fittick's Kirkyard. Suspicious of their real intentions, the landlady remarked that it seemed rather late at night to go buying cattle. Back came the sinister reply: "O', we'll buy you too, if you like".

'Rebells, Outlawis and Abortive Bairns'

The dark shape of the huge monumental crown of King's College, Aberdeen, silhouetted the night sky, but in the dimly-lit classroom a group of eager young students watched William Gordon anatomise the subject: a dog. Such was the enthusiasm for Gordon and his teachings, even although for the previous two years they had nothing to dissect but animals. Aberdeen had been the first British university to appoint a 'mediciner', a professor of medicine. James Cumyne became medical officer for Aberdeen burgh in 1503, and began teaching in King's College when it was completed two years later. Cambridge appointed a corresponding professorship in 1540, Oxford followed six years later. In Scotland the dates of similar appointments were made in Glasgow (1637), Edinburgh (1685) and St Andrews in 1721.

Anatomy had been carried out throughout Europe for many centuries before. Hippocrates had to face the same difficulties which befell future medical men because of public opinion against dissection of humans. Doctors who followed the Roman legions dissected the bodies of barbarians after battle.

The earliest teachings at most Scottish universities was probably based on the writings of Aristotle and Galen, but the students had to be content with examining the insides of beasts. In 1505 the earliest provision in Edinburgh for dissection was made, when the town council granted a charter to the Incorporation of Surgeons and Barbers whereby every entrant should, "knaw anatomea nature and complexioun of every member in manis bodie . . ." for which purpose we (the surgeons) may have "anis in the yeir ane condampnit man efter he be deid to mak anatomea of quhairthrow we may have had experience ilk ane to instruct uthers, and we sall do suffrage for the soule". So once a year the Edinburgh gallows proved a source of supply, however small. And take note the stipulated suffrage for the soul, indicating the persistence of the strong association between surgery and religion. In the surgical theatre the subject was carved into ten parts and distributed to ten members of the Incorporation, who dissected for private benefit or for the enlightenment of the apprentices.

The Edinburgh surgeons were thus restricted to one body a year until 1694, when an attempt was made to open an anatomical school in the Scottish capital. They received a further grant stating that "those bodies that dye in the correction house; the bodies of fundlings who dye betwixt the tyme that they are weaned and thir being put to schools or trades; also the dead bodies of such that are stiflet in the birth, which are exposed, and have none to owne them; as also the dead bodies of such as are *felo de se*; likewayes the bodies of such as are put to death by sentence of the magistrat". In 1695 the surgeons were given the power to examine all practising anatomy, surgery and pharmacy in the Lothians and Borders of Scotland.

The charter followed representations to the town council by Alexander Monteith, the famous physician, who wrote: "We seek the liberty of opening the bodies of poor persons who die in Paul's Workhouse, and have none to bury them; and also agree to wait on these poor for nothing, and bury them at our own charge, which now the town does. I do propose if this be granted to make better improvements in anatomy in a short time than have been made by Leyden in thirty years."

Aberdeen was lucky in having a man such as William Gordon as its 'mediciner' and in 1636 he successfully petitioned

the Privy Council for permission to teach human dissection.
Gordon had been a graduate of Padua, where the teachings of
a Belgian, Vesalius, had given the university as being the finest
medical school in Europe. Vesalius was to influence many with
his magnificent book, *The Fabric of the Human Body* which
was hailed as one of the finest achievements of science in modern
times.

Tired of dissecting dogs, Gordon petitioned the Lords who
directed the sheriffs and provosts of Aberdeen and Banff to
deliver annually to Gordon: "twa bodies of men, being notable
malefactors, executte in thair bonds, especiallie being rebells and
outlawis; and failseing of them, the bodies of the poorer sort,
dieing in hospitalls; or abortive bairns, foundlings or of those
of no qualitie, who has died of thare diseases, and hes few
friends or acquaintances than can tak exception". Apart from
being a distinguished surgeon, Gordon was an accomplished
architect and designed the King's College 'crown' after the
original was blown down by a gale in 1633.

The groan of the gallows was sweet music to the early anatomists and barber-surgeons of Scotland and England. But the
victims and their relatives were determined they should not
fall into the hands of the medical men. Hundreds of condemned
men and women who walked to the scaffold at Tyburn in
London or elsewhere were horrified in their last moments as to
what would happen to their remains after they had been cut
down. The Newgate Calendar, which was compiled by Old
Bailey attorney's-at-law and is a grim catalogue of the life and
death of prisoners in the notorious London jail of long ago, tells
of their fears.

A Smithfield butcher, Vincent Davis, arrested after stabbing
his wife to death, blurted out to the constables: "I have killed
the best wife in the world, and I am certain of being hanged,
but for God's sake, don't let me be anatomized!" After he was
sentenced to death Davis wrote appealing letters to friends,

begging them to rescue his body if any attempt should be made to 'snatch' it from the gallows. On the day of the execution, April 30, 1725, Davis walked to the scaffold "in the most gloomy and reserved manner". The Newgate Calendar further commented: "The anxiety this miserable wretch expressed for the care of his body, after having perpetrated such an unprovoked murder as he might well suppose would hazard the salvation of his soul, affords a melancholy picture how much concerned we can be for smaller matters to the neglect of the more important. It should teach us how superior the value of the soul is to that of a poor frail carcass; since the former must exist to all eternity, while the latter, in a few years at the most, will moulder into dust!" The Calendar does not record whether Davis got his wish, but with so much advance publicity it is doubtful.

The next of kin of two notorious criminals of the same period went to great lengths to cheat the surgeons. The Thief-Taker General, Jonathan Wild, was secretly buried in St Pancras' Churchyard after his execution at Tyburn, but his body was later exhumed. The highwayman Dick Turpin had a dread of being dissected. And after his execution at York in April 1739 his acquaintances took extraordinary precautions to save their hero's body. They eventually succeeded, even although his body was in the hands of the surgeons for a short while.

The Newgate Calendar tells how after the execution, the corpse was taken to the Blue Boar tavern in the town's Castlegate. The following morning Turpin was buried in the churchyard at St George's parish, with an inscription on the coffin, bearing his initials and age. The grave was made remarkably deep, but the following morning at three o'clock the coffin was empty. After a wide search the townsfolk found the highwayman's body hidden in a garden belonging to one of York's surgeons. Turpin was then laid on a makeshift stretcher and carried triumphantly through the streets by the mob. The body was put back in the coffin, which was filled with quick-lime and re-buried. Burglar John Barnet, caught breaking into a house at Peterhead, Aberdeenshire, was hanged at Aberdeen in the autumn of 1818. In a bid to beat the surgeons his friends buried Barnet at sea. But fate took a hand and his corpse was later washed up at the mouth of the River Don and handed over to the doctors.

In the autumn of 1750 a condemned Irishman, William Smith, the son of a priest, had the nerve to launch an appeal for public subscriptions to save his body. A part of his appeal which appeared in the newspapers reads: "As to my corporeal frame, it is unworthy of material notice; but, for the sake of that reputable family from whom I am descended, I cannot refrain from an anxiety when I think how easily this poor body, in my friendless and necessitious condition, may fall into the possession of the surgeons, and perpetuate my disgrace beyond the severity of the law. So great an impoverishment has my long confinement brought upon me, that I have not a shilling left for subsistence, much less for the procuring the decency of an internment. Therefore, I do most fervently entreat the generosity of the humane and charitably compassionate to afford me such a contribution as may be sufficient to protect my dead body from indecency, and to give me the consolation of being assured that my poor ashes shall be decently deposited within the limits of consecrated ground."

The blarney of the Irish won the hearts of the Londoners and enough money was collected to prevent his remains from falling into the wrong hands. But no doubt the wording of perhaps the strangest newspaper advertisement ever published, caught the eye of the early resurrectionists and Smith's body had probably not rested in peace for long. Sufficient to say the Irishman had been executed for committing fraud.

Soon after Smith's appeal the surgeons received an unexpected boost to the supply of bodies when in 1751 an act was passed

which decreed that executed murderers should either be publicly dissected or hung in chains or gibbets.

The bodies of murderers, if not gibbeted, were conveyed to
the nearest surgeons' hall, and it was ruled a felony if anyone
attempted to 'rescue' the bodies. The first to suffer under the
new act was a 17-year-old London youth, Thomas Wilford, who
slit the throat of his prostitute wife within a week of their
marriage. The judge pronounced, "you are to be taken to the
common place of execution, and there hanged by the neck until
you are dead; after which your body is to be publicly dissected
and anatomized, agreeably to an act of Parliament in that case
made and provided; and may God Almighty have mercy on
your soul".

Some criminals, faced with the choice between two evils,
considered dissection preferable to the indignity of rotting in
chains. Public dissection would appear to have been a swift
enough business, while some corpses hung in chains for years.
At Portsmouth, England, one villain swung so long on a gibbet
he was used as an additional navigation aid by the Royal Navy.

In Edinburgh there was the macabre case of Nichol Brown,
a criminal who had a taste for human flesh and for ill-treating
his wife. The depraved creature murdered the poor woman by
roasting her over the kitchen fire and was duly executed in
August 1754. Once on a drunken spree he boasted to his friends
that he would eat the flesh of a gibbeted man. Norman Ross,
hanged a week earlier, provided rich pickings and one night
Brown carried a portion of the dead man's leg back to a Leith
pub to put his mates off their ale by grilling a late night snack
over the fire.

Brown's own body did not hang about long after he was
gibbeted. It was stolen from its lofty perch and tossed into a
nearby pond. The pond was dragged and the body replaced on
the gibbet. But again it was stolen, and despite tempting re-
wards, it was never recovered. It is a safe bet that Nichol

Brown's body is not mouldering in some unknown grave; his skeleton would have proved useful to a surgeon.

Criminals were hung in chains in Scotland until the beginning of the nineteenth century. In 1810 a young man named Gillan was sentenced to death for raping and murdering a girl on the moor of Stynie, not far from Fochabers, Morayshire. The judge ordered that the execution should take place as near as possible to the spot where the girl's body was found and that Gillan be hung in chains "till the fowls of the air pick the flesh from your bones and the winds of Heaven bleach them white".

The murderer's corpse was stolen from the gallows, but for more than 100 years 'Gillan's Gallows' served as a macabre landmark to the peasants, who were said to be afraid to pass the execution spot at night because of the rattling and eerie whine of the chains. Nobody would dare to cut down the gallows, until, in 1911, the Duke of Gordon and Richmond issued orders to his estate workmen to take it down and bury it where it stood. During the excavation they discovered the bones of a man. It was concluded whoever cut down the body of Gillan had buried it at the foot of the gallows.

The Age of the Resurrectionists belonged to the first thirty years of the nineteenth century, with Scotland the chief theatre of the drama. This was because a strong belief in the resurrection of the body had been held in a strictly literal and material way by the Scots, and woe-betide anyone who dared shatter the peace of the grave.

Therefore, the Scots' repugnance to dissection of the human body, fortified by their religious beliefs, for centuries proved a barrier to anatomical research throughout the country. But despite these ever-present obstacles, the enthusiasm of the anatomists and their students refused to be stifled and the work progressed. Even so, in the early years Scots diplomas were regarded with contempt in England owing to the way in which degrees were often given by certain Scottish universities. Glasgow often gave degrees without requiring any certificate from the candidates of previous study.

St Andrews and Aberdeen were accused of trafficking in degrees in the eighteenth century. On one occasion St Andrews sold a degree to a stage doctor, and even Edinburgh added to the scandal by conferring an M.D. degree on an illiterate brushmaker. During this period men with ambition, or means, travelled abroad to study. To Paris, Utrecht, Gottingen and, above all, to the University of Leyden in Holland.

But the many truly eminent teachers who filled the medical and surgical chairs of Scottish universities in successive generations brought about an immense improvement in teaching methods and won for themselves and schools a European fame. In Edinburgh in 1750 there were about sixty medical students, being taught anatomy and swotting up crude prescriptions, which included ingredients such as spiders' webs, human blood, frogs, insects, and the excrement of horse, pig and even, peacock. In 1766 there were 160 students, but by 1800 the number had grown to 660—and still climbing.

The eighteenth-century resurrectionists faced unbending opposition from the public, and in Scotland there were many violent scenes involving both factions. In 1704 Edinburgh University appointed its first Professor of Anatomy, Mr Elliott, at a salary of £15 a year, and six years later there came the first outcry at body-snatching in the city. Following these complaints the Corporation of Surgeons recorded, "of late there has been a violation of sepulchres in the Greyfriars Churchyard" (the city's chief burial yard at that time) "by some who must unchristianly have been stealing the bodies of the dead".

The year 1724 was an important milestone in Edinburgh's medical history; Alexander Monro took over the professorial chair and for 126 years the Monro dynasty remained all-powerful as father followed son into the chair. The year after the first Monro took up office the College of Surgeons handed out a stiff warning to apprentices; their indentures would include a clause forbidding violation of graves. By 1725 Edinburgh's Chirurgeon Apothecaries were again trying to appease and reassure the country people and poor of the town, who were said to be "frightened by a villainous report that they are in danger of being attacked and seized by chirurgeons' apprentices".

Edinburgh was torn by riots in March 1742. The trouble erupted after the body of Alexander Baxter, buried a week before in the West Kirkyard, was discovered in a house next to the shop of a barber-surgeon, Martin Eccles. The grim discovery attracted a great mob, who seized the Portsburgh drum and marched down the Cowgate. The drum was eventually recovered by the militia, but not without a pitched battle during which the homes of several surgeons were attacked and the windows knocked in. But the mob did not give up so easily, and the following day they laid siege to Surgeon Eccles' shop. Again the mob were dispersed. The surgeon and his apprentice were brought before the magistrates, but freed because of lack of proof of body-stealing.

Four days after the riots, the Incorporation of Surgeons met "to testify their abhorrence of so wicked a crime" as body-snatching and warned apprentices they would forfeit their indentures and offered 100 merks reward for information leading to the discovery of resurrectionists. But the rioting was not over. On March 15 a rumour swept the city that one of the West Kirk beadles, a man called Haldane, was involved in grave-robbing activities. The rumour touched off two days of bloodshed and rioting and the beadle's house, dubbed 'Resurrectionist Hall', was destroyed by fire. The account of the raid in the *Scots Magazine* of 1742 gives the earliest known use of the word, 'resurrectionist'. On March 18 the outraged citizens marched on the home of a gardener, Richardson, who was thought to be involved in body-snatching, and his house was put to the torch. And before the month ended the hangman publicly burned a sedan chair in which a body had been found at the Nether Bow Port, and the two chairmen were banished from Edinburgh.

But the body-snatchers seemed not in the least bit disturbed by the rough-justice their contemporaries were receiving at the hands of the mob. Their nocturnal visits to the kirkyards went on. On April 6, 1743, a gardener from Grangegateside was stopped at the Potterrow Port by the city guard. In the sack he carried was the body of a child recently buried in Pentland Kirkyard. The High Court judge ordered the man to be whipped through the streets of Edinburgh and transported. Glasgow, too, had its share of trouble in the early days, and in 1749 several people were injured in a 'resurrectionist riot'.

Elsewhere in Scotland the activities of the body-snatchers seemed to go on unnoticed. Dissections were almost certainly carried out in Aberdeen after William Gordon's successful petition to the Lords, for in September 1741 part of King's College was referred to as the 'Anatomical Hall'.

But the menfolk did not have it all their own, gory way. In February 1752, Scotland's first, and only 'Resurrectionist Women' were caught in Edinburgh. The ghastly case of Helen Torrence and Jean Waldie shocked the country. The drunken pair appeared before the High Court on a charge of plagium, 'man-stealing'. They had agreed to hand over to a surgeon the body of a child, but failed to do so. Instead they stole and killed another and sold it to the anatomist for 2s 6d and the price of a dram. There was little sympathy for them on the walk to the gallows.

Dead and Buried . . . ?

—

A tombstone in the kirkyard at Inverurie in rural Aberdeen-shire commemorates a woman who was the victim of an early resurrectionist—and lived to tell the tale! She was Marjorie Elphinstone, the wife of Walter Innes of Ardtannies, which was a small estate on the banks of the River Don, a mile from the market town. Marjorie 'died' in the first decade of the seventeenth century and being the wife of a wealthy landowner she was interred wearing her jewellery. Word got round the parish of the 'buried treasure' and on the night after the funeral the gravedigger opened the grave and began to tear the rings from the woman's fingers. In so doing, he roused Marjorie from a coma, and her first sleepy groan sent him scurrying from the burial ground.

After recovering her jewellery Marjorie walked back along the track the funeral cortege had taken earlier in the day. When she reached Ardtannies she beat on the door. Inside her grief-stricken husband was being consoled by relatives. When she knocked again her husband said had he not seen his wife 'kistit and happit' he would have sworn it was her knock.

Marjorie died in 1622, having survived her husband by six years, as proved by the quaintly-decorated tombstone at Inverurie. The stone was originally displayed inside the old kirk, which was demolished in 1775.

An Orcadian woman, Margaret Halcrow, the wife of Rev. Henry Erskine, the minister of Chirnside in the Scottish

Lothians, was also buried alive for a short spell. They married in
1674 and she was his second wife, but 'died' soon after. Like
Marjorie Elphinstone, the minister's wife was buried with her
jewellery. The sexton purposely filled in her grave lightly then
later dug her up and tried to cut off her ring finger. She
screamed with pain, leapt out of her coffin and, with shroud
flapping in the night air, hurried to the manse. She knocked
loudly at the front door, and it is little wonder her husband was
scared out of his wits when he heard her voice implore: "Open
the door, for I'm fair clemmed wi' the cauld." Margaret lived
to do a great service for the church in Scotland, for she became
the mother of Ralph and Ebenezer Erskine, founders of the
original Secession Church of Berwickshire.

Grave-robbing had been a lucrative business from the days
of the Ancient Egyptians, with grave-diggers sharing in the
spoils with robbers. Orem in his *Book of Old Aberdeen* tells of
a seventeenth-century beadle at St Machar's Cathedral who
sifted through the bones and ashes of the dead to rob them of
their jewellery.

Condemned men and women were haunted by 'miracle'
revivals, such as occurred in Inverurie and Chirnside. For they
had a terrible dread that the hangman would bungle the job
and that they would hang in a state of suspended animation
until handed over to the surgeon to be cut up alive! 'Half-
Hangit' Maggie Dickson of Musselburgh was one of the lucky
ones. She was executed in Edinburgh's Grassmarket in 1728,
then cut down and coffined. The mob helped relatives in a gruesome tug-o'-war with medical students over her body, and there
was a stand-up fight under the shadow of the gallows.

After a short, bloody struggle the mob won, and the horse-
drawn cart carrying Maggie headed for the Honest Toun of
Musselburgh. And as it rattled over the cobbles of the town,
nine miles from Edinburgh, Maggie came back to life. 'Half-
Hangit' Maggie became a source of pride to many locals and

she was pointed out to visiting strangers. She also lived for many years and had a large number of children.

Execution by hanging in those days was carried out differently from the procedure adopted by hangmen before the abolition of capital punishment in Britain; there was no sudden drop into eternity. The victim mounted a ladder, or stood on a bucket, and had the feet kicked from beneath him. Hence the saying, 'to kick the bucket'. A hangman's ladder, last used in 1722, is stored in ancient St Magnus' Cathedral at Kirkwall, Orkney.

In the sixteenth century there was the harrowing case of a murderer who was hanged in London but came to life as he was being wheeled through the streets to the Chirurgeons' Hall in the city's Cripplegate. It happened in 1587 and is recorded in Stow's Annals: "The 20 of Februarie, a strange thing happened a man hanged for felonie at Saint Thomas Waterines, being begged by the Chirurgeons of London, to have made of him an anatomie, after he was dead to all men's thinking, cut downe, throwne into a carre, and so brought from the place of execution through the Borough of Southwarke over the bridge, and through the Citie of London to the Chirurgeons Hall nere unto Cripelgate: The chest being opened there, and the weather extreme cold hee was found to be alive, and lived till the three and twentie of Februarie, and then died."

The barber-surgeons, anxious that such a thing would not be repeated, ruled that any members who did so would face a fine and pay any expenses involved.

In Scotland, too, there is evidence that the grim work of the hangman was not always completely satisfactory. In February 1678 four vagabonds from a family called Shaw, the father and three sons, were hanged in Edinburgh for slaughtering members of the rival Faws tribe in a drunken brawl. The two sides had met to discuss a tribal battle against the Browns and Baillies and to chase them back to Ireland. But the Shaws and Faws fell out with each other, and the city guard made a number of arrests.

After the bodies were cut down from the scaffold the four Shaws were thrown into a pit in Greyfriars Churchyard. But the next morning the youngest of the three sons (he was barely 16, according to contemporary records) had vanished. The Fountainhall MS, which was handed down to the Faculty of Advocates at Edinburgh, gives this theory for his disappearance: "Some thought he being last thrown over the ladder, and first cut downe, and in full vigour, and no great heap of earth, and lying upper-most, and so not so ready to smother, the fermentation of the blood, and heat of the bodies under him, might cause him to rebound and throw off the earth, and recover ere the morning, and steall away; which, if true, he deserves his life, tho' the magistrates, or their bourreau, deserved a reprimande; but others, more probably, thought his body was stolen away by some chirurgeon, or his servant to make ane anatomicale dissection on; which was criminal to take it at their owne hand, since the magistrat's would not have refused it."

The fear of being dissected alive was heightened following the unusual case of William Duell, who came back to life as he was being prepared for the anatomist after his execution at Tyburn in November 1740. Duell, who was hanged for raping and murdering Sarah Griffin at Acton, was taken to the barber-surgeons' hall and immediately stripped and washed. Five minutes after he was stretched out on the table the anatomist's assistant noticed that Duell was breathing slowly and his pulse faint. In less than two hours he was able to sit up in a chair and drink wine, although still in great pain.

The Sheriffs ordered that Duell be carried back to Newgate Prison. Four days later Duell was the star prisoner and was able to eat, drink and talk to visitors and fellow prisoners. But he was unable to recollect the events after he stood on the scaffold. He was later given a reprieve and was transported for life. The cost of the abortive anatomical demonstration can still be found in the barber-surgeon company's accounts. It totalled £5 16s, which included a fee of 5s to a charwoman who washed the 'body'.

At the beginning of 1803 the public were haunted by a living nightmare. They were left to decide whether a condemned man was alive or dead when he was dissected. George Foster was executed in the Old Bailey for the murder of his wife and child. Cut down by the hangman, he was brought to the rooms of Professor Aldini to be experimented upon with electrical apparatus. The Newgate Calendar takes up the tale of terror as the Professor subjected the body to galvanic process: "On the first application of the process to the face, the jaw of the deceased criminal began to quiver, and the adjoining muscles were horribly contorted, and one eye was actually opened", observed the writer. "In the subsequent part of the process, the right hand was raised and clenched, and the legs and thighs were set in motion." Observers turned white with fear as they watched the experiment, and some thought Foster was coming back to life. The terrifying experience proved too much for Mr Pass, the beadle of the surgeons' company. He was so alarmed by what he saw that he died of fright soon after returning home. The Newgate Calendar scoffed at the idea that the dead man could be revived. "This was impossible, as several of his friends who were under the scaffold had pulled violently his legs, in order to put a more speedy termination to his sufferings." But maybe they did not 'pull his leg' hard enough!

There was a similar horrifying experiment in Glasgow in November 1818, when a university lecturer, Andrew Ure, carried out tests in galvanism on a murderer called Clydesdale. The killer had sold his body the day before his execution. After he had dangled on the scaffold for an hour Clydesdale's corpse was rushed to the university where Ure attached it to a Voltaic pile. Ure failed to revive Clydesdale but the corpse's contortions sent spectators scurrying from the room in horror. In 1819 electricity was used to bring round a person who had fallen into the Clyde. And in recent years there have been instances in the city where people thought to be dead later came to life. One man who collapsed in the street actually came round on the mortuary slab, an identification label tied to his big toe!

In eighteenth-century Germany a condemned man was not so lucky. He was a notorious criminal who after his execution was handed over to the surgeons. As he lay on the table the operator felt life in the body. According to the Newgate Calendar he addressed his fellow doctors: "I am pretty certain, gentlemen, from the warmth of the subject and the flexibility of the limbs, that by a proper degree of attention and care the vital heat would return, and life in consequence take place. But when it is considered what a rascal we should again have among us, that he was hanged for so cruel a murder, and that, should we restore him to, life, he would probably kill somebody else." And, with a final glance at his colleagues, he added, "I say, gentlemen, all these things considered, it is my opinion that we had better proceed in the dissection."

The Dog-Cart Men

Sea fog spread cold, clinging tentacles through the narrow, cobbled streets of the Firth of Forth village, as the two well-dressed strangers in the dog-cart drove up to the inn. They were greeted by an ostler whom they told to feed and water the horse, while they went inside for a refreshment.

During the half-hour or so they spent in the pub, the strangers informed the ostler they were expecting a parcel to be delivered by a servant and that it would be put in the box under the seat. The landlord accepted his customers' offer of a dram, and they struck up a conversation. The main topic at the inn was the notoriety the village had thrust upon it as the result some weeks before of the death of a boy who had died of hydrocephalus; water on the brain. They learned that while alive the boy had attracted the attention of doctors from as far away as Edinburgh; and the villagers had feared an attempt by medical students to wrench the body from the local graveyard. Every night since the funeral the fisherfolk had shared watches in the cemetery to prevent such an outrage.

The strangers lit up expensive-looking cigars then left the inn, explaining they were going for a short walk. They informed the ostler again to look-out for their servant. About half-an-hour later a man in scarlet livery arrived at the inn, carrying a bulky package which he placed in the boot. Shortly afterwards, the two strangers returned, got into the dog-cart and drove off in the direction of Edinburgh.

Darkness gripped the village and it was time for the watchmen to mount guard over the boy's grave. But when they got there they found it open and the body decapitated. The angry villagers headed for the inn as word got around about the strangers. It was then that the ostler declared that he had seen a flash of scarlet under the overcoat of one of the gentlemen as he clambered into the cart before leaving. And he recalled how after the servant locked the parcel in the boot he had taken the key away in his pocket.

That night a big manhunt was mounted in surrounding hamlets and townships in an effort to trace the impudent resurrectionists. By the next morning the clues led the village minister and dominie to Edinburgh. Dr Alexander Monro, Professor of Anatomy at the university, and the third member of his family to occupy the chair, was questioned about the disappearance, but could not help. Next on their calling list was Dr John Barclay, a famous extra-mural lecturer on anatomy and physiology in Surgeons' Square.

Barclay could not help, but invited the visitors to search his anatomical theatre and rooms, which they did without success. The crest-fallen villagers returned home; and a rare anatomical specimen remained in Edinburgh. For the two travellers in the dog-cart were Robert Liston, who later became famous throughout the world of medicine, and Benjamin Crouch, the infamous London body-snatcher, who had fled to Scotland to become chief assistant to the great anatomist, and instruct students in the art of body-snatching.

Together, in less than half an hour, in daylight, or at best in gathering dusk, they had robbed a grave that had baffled the best of Scotland's professional body-snatchers. Liston, brash, arrogant, but brilliant, had no doubt hatched the daring scheme, choosing the one man who could have helped carry it out in such short time and under such conditions. They had to burrow through six feet of earth, welded together by weeks of rainfall; then smash open a strongly carpentered coffin to reach the body and get completely away without being spotted. But they accomplished the plot. When they set off for their stroll round the village they had made straight for the cemetery. After exhuming the body one of the men pulled off his travelling coat assuming disguise of a liveried servant and carried the parcel, previously hidden, to the cart. Then returned to his companion to dress himself.

The incongruous partnership of Liston and the 'Corpse-King' was a sign of the times; the need of the anatomists to employ men such as Crouch to keep the source of bodies flowing. Liston was a son of the manse; his father being the minister of Ecclesmachan in the Lothians. The young Liston did brilliantly at school and later at Edinburgh University, where he became a useful Latin scholar. He adopted surgery as his profession and in later years became a member of the Council and of the Board of Examiners of the Royal College of Surgeons in England and a Fellow of the Royal Society.

He returned to Edinburgh in 1818 and stayed for ten years. He gained a great reputation as an operating surgeon and anatomist, but his manner made him many enemies. In 1822 he was involved in a head-on clash with the authorities and expelled from the Royal Infirmary. By 1834, he became surgeon at the newly-founded hospital attached to London University and the next year was appointed Professor of Clinical Surgery at the University of London.

Liston had the reputation of being one of the foremost surgeons in Europe; it was a reputation hard won.

When he returned from London in 1818 his two rivals, Dr Monro and Dr Barclay, and their pupils had a good thing going on the body-snatching front by dividing up graveyards in towns and villages between them, and did not stray into each others' territories. Liston refused to recognise any territorial rights and this led to stand-up fights among the tombstones. He was fearless and had a powerful physique to back up any argument. He was so strong he could immobilise a struggling man's leg with one hand and saw it off with the other. He also has a place in the present-day record books. *The Guinness Book of Records* notes that the shortest time for the amputation of a limb in the pre-anaesthetic era was a mere 33 seconds through a patient's thigh by Robert Liston. The lightning feat unfortunately caused his assistant the loss of three fingers from his master's saw! It was said by his contemporaries that when he amputated, "the gleam of his knife was followed so instantaneously by the sound of sawing as to make the two actions appear almost simultaneous".

Legends of his body-snatching exploits spread through the medical fraternity of Scotland. His students worshipped him, and deemed it a great honour to go on a midnight raid with him. On one occasion he led a party of students in the quest of a number of freshly-buried corpses in an Edinburgh churchyard. They dug quickly and expertly and within a short space of time they had exhumed two corpses, stripped them of their shrouds, and re-buried the empty coffins. They had been digging into a third grave, when the student look-out shouted a warning.

Suddenly, the Liston gang were surrounded by an angry mob, some armed with shot-guns and blunderbusses. Amid shots and whistling buckshot the resurrectionists scattered. But Liston delayed only for a few seconds to scoop up the two naked bodies, one under each brawny arm, and dash for a small doorway in the cemetery wall. He fastened the door behind him, and lay hidden in a private garden nearby until dawn when he slipped away. Later that day two porters arrived at the spot to carry the 'things' back to Liston.

One dark night Liston and Ben Crouch were on the prowl but as they neared the burial yard, they could hear angry voices and see the glimmer of lanterns. Crouch retraced his footsteps to the roadway, on Liston's orders, while the surgeon pressed on to the cemetery. Hidden behind a tombstone he listened as two rival parties of resurrectionists argued over the ownership of the body in the open coffin.

As the argument raged and developed into a scuffle, Liston, dressed in bible black, rose from his hiding spot with a demoniacal scream. The frightened body-snatchers did not stop to lift the corpse as they dashed from the scene. The surgeon grabbed the opportunity, and, of course, the body.

Liston was one of the first to go in search of bodies across the Forth and was involved in several adventures. There was the time he and his team hired a boat and headed for Fife after they had heard that a young sailor had been buried in the lonely cemetery between Limekilns and Rosyth. When they reached the rocky shore they quickly clambered up the eight-foot dyke that barred their way to the cemetery. The place was unguarded, but they were presented with a completely unexpected hindrance. The sailor's sweetheart kneeled weeping and crooning beside the grave on which she had strewn wild flowers.

They waited patiently for dusk to fall, then the stricken girl left the scene. It was time for the resurrectionists to swoop, and within a short time the body was in a sack and on its way back across the Forth. As they rowed away they heard a cry and through the gathering darkness they could see the girl running about the cemetery in a demented state. But the tragic scene did not seem to bother Liston and his students. They were well-pleased with the 'snatch', and were wearing buttonholes of the flowers the grief-stricken girl had placed on her sweetheart's grave only a short time before.

On another occasion at Culross, Fife, the Edinburgh anatomist and Crouch disguised themselves as sailors and retired for a drink in the village inn, first leaving the body in a sack behind a hedge. As they were sipping their whisky, the door of the inn was thrown open and in staggered the barmaid's brother, a sailor on leave. He was very drunk and over a shoulder was slung a familiar-looking sack. He explained he had found it behind the hedge, then proceeded to cut the cord round the mouth of the sack. The jolly sailor and his sister screamed with horror when the dead man's grey hair popped out. As they ran from the room into the adjoining kitchen, Liston seized the chance to get clean away with his students.

Liston seldom came off second best. But it did happen. In a churchyard on the outskirts of Edinburgh he and his ever-faithful companion, Ben Crouch, were about to raise a body when they were disturbed by a medical student, Mowbray Thomson, one of Dr Barclay's boys. The odds seemed hopeless, but Thomson was determined to baulk Liston and calmly produced a pistol. He threatened to fire into the air and alert the neighbourhood. As Thomson's colleagues arrived at the grave, Liston anxiously looked at his watch and decided to leave the field to the young students.

With 900 medical students in Edinburgh at that time, few graveyards escaped the attention of the resurrectionists. Many of the students found the business a difficult game to play, and some were unwilling. In Aberdeen reluctant students were fined. A local surgeon moved that "every person absenting himself from depositing or taking up a dead body should be fined 10s 6d, unless indisposed". Their colleagues shared the fines and the doctors also paid them each a shilling to "warm the inside of your jacket".

The amateur-body-snatchers found it a frightening game, too. Three young students discovered this fact when they went by gig to rob a woman's grave at Penicuik, near Edinburgh. One remained on guard beside the hired gig, while his companions climbed over a wall. After wrenching open the exhumed coffin they realised they had not brought a sack or chest in which to carry away the body. Neither fancied stripping the body, so they foolishly decided to leave it in its shroud. If they had been caught, they would have been charged with stealing the shroud, and this could have cost them a jail sentence.

They were new at the business and were anxious to quit the graveyard. One of the students threw the body over his shoulder and made for the gates. As he trotted towards the gig, the body he was carrying began to slip. He lost his terrified grip on the shroud, and finally its feet touched the ground. The student's hair bristled as he became aware of the shuffling of feet behind him, and the knees of the corpse began to touch the back of his calves. He imagined the corpse was moving on its own accord. Sobbing hysterically, he threw the body to the ground, then leapt into the gig shouting: "She's alive! She's alive! My God, She's alive!" His friends did not dally to investigate. The following morning the astonished husband of the dead woman thought his wife had made an effort to return from the dead when he found her body in the roadway.

Animals, as in the early days of anatomy, were still in demand. Surgeons paid 2s 6d for a dog, and the supply was plentiful. Tammas, the fictional hero of Grant's *The Chronicle of Keckleton*, became a sworn enemy of the local practitioner, Dr Lott, after his pet cat, Black Tam, vanished.

Tammas had absolutely no proof that the doctor or his family were to blame, but he warned his wife: "There's nae a cat nor a dog can gang in the direction o' the Back Lodge, let alone enterin' the grounds roon' the lodge, that ever finds its way hame again; but it's well kent where the puir brutes gang, even to Dr Lott's Burkin' House; as what used to be the laundry at Back Lodge is very properly noo ca'd. Tak' ye my word for't, Marget, Dr Lott an' his students dinna content themsel's wi' the mere dissection o' brute beasts, but mony a graif has had to render up its deid to their scalpels as weel."

Parisian students often had to rely on the guillotine for a supply of specimens (1803)

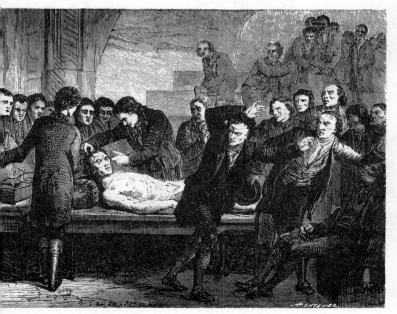

Ure galvanising the body of the murderer Clydesdale (Glasgow 1818)

Bodysnatchers at work (*from a contemporary engraving*).
Note the rival gang in the background ready to move in
and steal the corpse

The churchyard at Banchory-Devenick, Kincardineshire

The watch-house and iron coffin (right)

PLATE 3

The watchtower in the graveyard at Banchory-Ternan
Note the table-top gravestones

PLATE 4

To Rob A Grave

—

Body-snatching is a lost art. For many years the methods of the body-snatchers remained a mystery, and the greatest puzzle to outsiders was how the resurrectionists were able to operate so quickly. The speed with which bodies were exhumed was simply breath-taking. There were instances where two bodies were whipped from separate graves of considerable depth in just 90 minutes and another where the corpse was removed from a shallow grave in quarter-of-an-hour.

In the early days of the body-snatchers the grave was opened, the body wrenched from the shattered coffin, and then the raiders fled, leaving the open grave behind. But in the succeeding years they restored the grave to its original condition, replacing the last turf carefully. This was not done out of consideration for the feelings of the family of the dead person, but as an elaborate precaution against discovery, and so that they would be able to return to the graveyard again and again. If the relatives did not suspect that their kirkyard was being violated they would relax their guard, or, perhaps, even not bother to mount one.

The equipment of the body-snatchers consisted of smocks, lantern, ropes, hooks, a ladder, sometimes a fire-arm, and, of course, shovels. No ordinary spade was used. They preferred short, wooden spades, usually dagger-shaped. These ensured speedier, almost noiseless digging, with no chink of metal against stone. Corpses were carried off in sacks, tea chests, and, in later years, the snatchers became sophisticated and some

favoured a green baize cloth which they tied crossed corners.
After one unsuccessful raid by Aberdeen students on the lonely
Deeside graveyard at Coull, three miles from Aboyne, Aberdeenshire, they left behind a pickaxe, spade, screwdriver and a
telescopic pole with a hook on the end. The hook was probably
used to fish the body from the coffin as it lay in the grave. It
was during this particular raid that a young doctor was so badly
beaten by parishioners that he was crippled for life. Soon after
the incident the gravedigger, who was thought to be involved
in the plot to raise the dead, left the parish. In eighteenth-
century Aberlour, Banffshire, a doctor named MacPherson went
through life with a stiff arm, said to have been the result of an
injury he suffered as a student while trying to escape watchmen.

If they robbed a grave in town it was essential to carry a sack;
the body could be dumped in an old ruin or near the cemetery
to be collected the following day. Sometimes a getaway coach
was used, but this could attract attention if spotted by a night
watchman on his rounds. One inquisitive man opened the coach
door to find two bodies inside. The police were waiting for the
resurrectionists as they tumbled over the graveyard wall with a
third body.

The first rule of the body-snatcher when he reached the grave
he intended to rob was to memorise the area; no one must know
he had been there. As the toll of body-snatching mounted, so
relatives who could not afford a mort-safe, would scatter pebbles
or sea shells, flowers or twigs over the top of the grave. To any
one else the material would go un-noticed, but the resurrectionists knew of these markers, and that each day relations would
examine the objects to make sure the grave had not been rifled.
If they were careful they would operate freely in one particular
cemetery for long enough. But if the parishioners became suspicious this would mean the loss of a good 'pitch'. After body-
stealers had been disturbed at Kirkmichael in Ayrshire in

March 1829, a check revealed that twenty-two bodies had disappeared from their graves over a short period.

Whenever the mourners had left the graveside after a funeral, a 'spy' would go to the spot and make a mental note of any obstacles facing his colleagues. That night when the gang arrived they knew exactly what had to be done. In Scotland the time chosen to strike in the dark, winter nights was from six to eight o'clock, just before the kirkyard watch arrived and the police went on duty. At the grave, the students would first carefully remove every pebble, twig and such like, and set these aside. Then a hole was dug down to the coffin only where the head and shoulders lay. A canvas sheet was spread out to collect the soil, and on reaching the head of the coffin, two broad hooks or a crowbar were used to prise open the lid, which snapped against the weight of earth on the uncovered two-thirds of the cask. Sacking was used to deaden the sound of tearing wood.

Next, the body was fished out with hooks, stripped and the shroud pushed back into the coffin, to avoid a charge of theft. The body was then doubled in half, trussed, and put in the sack. The earth was tipped from the canvas sheet back into the grave, and any tell-tale pebbles or twigs replaced, along with the last sod. The whole job was usually completed within an hour, depending on how many men helped in the operation.

Dr Henry Lonsdale, pupil and colleague of Dr Knox, the Edinburgh anatomist, describes one method used. "In the disinternment of bodies considerable force was required, and this was mainly exerted round the neck by means of a cord and other appliances. Now, withdrawing the contents of a coffin by a narrow aperture was by no means an easy process, particularly at dead of night and whilst the actors were in a state of trepidation; a jerking movement is said to have been more effective than violent dragging."

Before the secrets of the body-snatchers were poured out to

Warburton's select committee, many ingenious theories of techniques were put forward by people who had never taken part in expeditions. Such an explanation was published in *The Lancet* in 1823 by its founder, Thomas Wakley. "In the case of a neat, or not quite new grave, the ingenuity of the Resurrectionist came into play. Several feet, fifteen or twenty, away from the head or foot of the grave, he would remove a square of turf, about eighteen or twenty inches in diameter. This he would carefully put by, and then commence to mine. Most pauper graves were of the same depth, and, if the sepulchre was that of a person of importance, the depth of the grave could be pretty well estimated by the nature of the soil thrown up. Taking a five-foot grave, the coffin lid would be about four feet from the surface. A rough slanting tunnel, some five yards long, would, therefore have to be constructed, so as to impinge exactly on the coffin head. This being at last struck (not very simple task), the coffin was lugged up by hooks to the surface, or preferably, the end of the coffin was wrenched off with hooks while still in the shelter of the tunnel, and the scalp or feet of the corpse secured through the open end, and the body pulled out, leaving the coffin almost intact and unmoved. The body once obtained, the narrow shaft was easily filled up and the sod of the turf accurately replaced. The friends of the deceased, seeing that the earth over his grave was not disturbed, would flatter themselves that the body had escaped the Resurrectionist; but they seldom noticed the neatly-placed square of turf some feet away."

Bransby Cooper, the nephew of the famous Sir Astley Cooper, was also given the 'secret' by a man claiming to be a friend of resurrectionists, although he had never joined them on their raids.

"Commencing their operations towards the head of the coffin, in a portion of the earth below the level of the mound, or raised portion of the grave, they rapidly made an excavation of such a diameter as only just to admit of the throwing out of the mould. As soon as the head of coffin was arrived at, and exposed, it was at once prised out; and that there was not much difficulty in doing this was shown to me, from the circumstances that the dependance for the security of the body was chiefly placed in the coffin lid, to the fastenings of which the attention of the undertaker was usually in particular directed.

"At this stage of the proceedings, however, a difficulty at once suggested itself, which evidently an unitiated person would, in all probability, have failed to surmount; for, as is well-known, the head of a coffin, as ordinarily constructed, is one of its narrowest portions, and never of such a width as to admit, in a direct manner, of the exit of the chest and shoulders of the corpse within. My informant however overcame this impediment at once, by describing the Resurrectionists as rounding the shoulders well over the chest, and then, in drawing out the body, giving to it such a general turn as to be enabled at once to extract it in a diagonal of the opening already described. By these means, I was informed two or more subjects could be extracted without much increase of time or labour, out of one and the same grave."

Sir Astley's nephew, his biographer, believed for many years that this was the method carried out. Years later, when the Anatomy Act had put an end to the corpse trade, Bransby was told by an old body-snatcher: "That would never do, sir. We should be working in old instead of the new soft ground. Besides it would be detected at once, for we could not do it without lengthening the grave."

The body-snatchers jealously guarded the secrets of their craft, and fed only snippets of information to the inquisitive. But we have some idea how they worked, and how quickly they could clean out a grave, sometimes several in one night. One man told the Select Committee in 1828 that he had dug up twenty-three bodies in four nights. Sometimes, as the result of an epidemic, several coffins were piled one upon the other in the grave. The method employed here is outlined by one London surgeon: "It sometimes happened, more especially when any epidemic had been committing extensive ravages in the population, that three or four coffins would be placed one upon another in the same grave and at the same time."

He added: "Under these circumstances, if the Resurrectionist wished to extract all the bodies, it was absolutely necessary that the whole of the newly-piled earth should be thrown out from the grave, the body removed, and the coffin taken up. Each coffin was thus raised in succession, and afterwards again deposited in the same order in which it had previously lain, and, finally, the earth was carefully restored with every possible exactitude, to accord with the form it had presented before its disturbance."

Body-snatching was made easy in instances where gravediggers and undertakers were themselves directly responsible. Such a person was Joseph Naples, a member of the Borough Gang, a highly-organised team of resurrectionists whose leader was Ben Crouch. Naples, the son of a stationer and bookbinder, ran off to sea and served on board *HMS Excellent* at the battle of Cape St Vincent. On leaving the navy he got a job as gravedigger at Spa Fields burial ground in London. For three years he made a considerable amount of money lifting bodies. At first he was reluctant, but, egged on by another gravedigger, he began stealing the bodies of babies, before graduating to adults.

Naples' method was simple. After the funeral he would unscrew the coffin lid, then lay the coffin in the grave. He would pretend to shovel earth, and, as soon as he thought he was unobserved, he would lower himself into the hole, extract the body and pop it into a sack. He would fill the grave with earth, at each stage lifting the sack near the surface. The body would only be a few inches below the surface when the job was done. He lost his position at Spa Fields when he was denounced by Ben Crouch. In May 1802 Naples was imprisoned for two years in the Middlesex House of Correction in Coldbathfields, but he escaped and was later recaptured. Sir Astley Cooper personally intervened with the Secretary of State, and after Naples was released he became a full-time resurrectionist. He remained a faithful servant of Sir Astley's until drink and the rigours of his ghoulish trade spirited him away.

At Glenbervie in the Kincardineshire Mearns, the parish minister, Rev. James Drummond, turned detective when a grave was robbed in his kirkyard, and suspicion fell heavily on John Clark, the faithful gravedigger and beadle, whose family had been connected with the church and its offices for generations. The parishioners were so outraged at Clark that the elders threatened to resign, unless he was punished.

But Rev. Drummond pointed out the nature of the earth around the violated grave. Clark, when digging a grave, always followed the same ritual by piling the earth on a particular side. The grave-robbers had been less careful and had dumped the earth on the other side. Clark was cleared and a scandal averted.

Undertakers were paid large bribes to provide weak fastenings on coffins. Sometimes the body-snatcher would act as the under-taker's assistant, who would collect the body from the death house. Common lodging houses provided a rich source, with resurrectionists impersonating the relatives of the dead person and then stealing the corpse as it awaited burial. Mortuaries and outhouses used for storing suicide victims prior to a cor-oner's inquest were burgled. But not all unscrupulous under-takers escaped the law. One Edinburgh police officer tracked down the body of an executed criminal stolen from an under-taker's premises after the undertaker had tipped off the snatchers. They carried the body off from an outhouse during the night and sold it to a surgeon. The policeman found the missing body in a dissecting room and was able to identify it by an unusual tattoo. The policeman was rewarded with an in-scribed silver stick for a great piece of detection, and the under-taker was jailed.

Bodies, Bells . . .

Rich or poor, it made no difference to the body-snatchers. In the early years of the nineteenth century, unprotected graves, whether those of a prince or pauper, provided a steady source of supply. But as their activities intensified, so determined efforts were made to keep them at bay. In the beginning, the poor sprinkled the graves of their kinsfolk with markers, but when this failed, they mixed clumps of heather or thatch into the earth to try and prevent digging. Quick lime in the coffin was an early answer, but this method was frowned upon for religious reasons.

But the Kirk or the local laird came to the aid of the poor of parishes by providing huge stone slabs to lay on top of the coffins. Later these were replaced by heavy iron-grilled mortsafes which encaged the coffin until it was beyond dissection. The mort-safe was removed from the grave for the next funeral. For many years a huge granite slab was used at Kemnay, in the Garioch district of Aberdeenshire. It measured more than six feet long, ten inches thick and was coffin-shaped. The Kemnay stone was to provide the grave-diggers with a puzzle. They found a carpet of dead leaves sandwiched between the stone and the top of a coffin. They were mystified until it was recalled that some weeks before there had been a great storm after the last internment. They concluded the leaves had blown into the open grave when an attempt was made to lift the stone by resurrectionists.

At Aberlour in Banffshire another mystery faced modern

gravediggers when, in March 1915, a grilled mort-safe was unearthed under which lay a coffin, apparently untouched and in good condition. But on being opened the coffin was found to be empty. Iron mort-safes, nicknamed 'Irons' in North-east Scotland, were also popular. A Cults builder George Barclay gifted two iron shells, each weighing 19 cwt, to Banchory-Devenick churchyard in Kincardineshire. Block and tackle were used to lower the shell into the grave, and removed after six weeks. A mort-safe was last used in the quaint churchyard in 1854, but it was not the solid-iron coffin, which can still be seen in a corner of the cemetery. The father of one young man had been a 'watcher o'er the dead' and was so frightened his son's body would be claimed by body-snatchers. Even although their activities had long passed, he instructed that two huge mort stones be placed over his son's coffin. The stones were unearthed in 1911 when a fresh grave was being dug.

Years later iron shells and mort-safes found a place in museums. But in the Aberdeen area the solid iron coffins found a more practical use on farms. They were used as cattle troughs. One such trough at Maryculter, Aberdeenshire, was nicknamed, 'The Coffin'.

The massive mort-safes proved efficient, but troublesome to the living who had to manhandle them before and after funerals. Mort-safe tackle which was used at Inverurie, Aberdeenshire, is now in the town museum. But during resurrectionist times the heavy, iron hooks, chains and sheerpoles were stored in a baker's shop. The bakehouse was picked because it meant the equipment would be under observation during both day and night. At the Quaker cemetery at Kinmuck, Aberdeenshire, it was said ten men were required to lift or lower the grilled, clamlike mort-safe. There was also a trick lock should the snatchers get deep enough. One half of the safe is now in Aberdeen University's anatomical department.

Table-topped gravestones proved decorative, but were not the absolute deterrent. Barred and grilled tombs were much used and the cemeteries and kirkyards of Scotland soon resembled zoological gardens. A massive 'cheese-dish' shaped mort-safe in the churchyard at Colinton in the Lothians was probably responsible for firing young Robert Louis Stevenson's imagination of the activities of resurrectionists. His grandfather, Lewis Balfour, was the parish minister and Stevenson used to play around the moulding tombstones. Perhaps his grandfather's tales gave him the idea for his chilling short story, 'The Body-snatcher'. He set the grave-robbing scene in the kirkyard at Glencorse.

The difficulties involved with mort-safes led to the introduction of burial vaults. At Udny, 14 miles north of Aberdeen, there is a most unusual vault; conical-shaped, slated with two doors—an inner and outer door, which is made of a double thickness of stout oak and strengthened with iron bolts. On the day of the funeral the coffin was placed on an oaken segmented platform which was then rotated slowly to make space for the next coffin. When the first body had made a full cycle of the vault and re-appeared in its coffin at the doorway it was ripe for burial.

The vault was completed just as the Anatomy Act became law. The idea for the vault was born on 21 January 1832 when fifteen Udny gentlemen, led by the parish minister, Rev. John Leslie, met at the Green of Udny "for the purpose of taking into consideration the propriety of erecting a vault in the churchyard for depositing the bodies of the dead previous to internment".

A plan was submitted by Mr Marr of Cairnbrogie, and the job was carried out by a mason Alexander Wallace of Smiddy-hole and wright Thomas Simpson of Oldmeldrum. The cost of construction was £114, although £5 had earlier been deducted from the mason's account because it was thought he did not conform to the contract.

But the running of the Udny vault had its problems. At the
first meeting at Udny Green the new committee ruled that the
amount of subscription entitling the subscriber to the right of
the vault would be indefinite but in cases where the committee
regarded such sum as trifling, or not nearly in proportion to the
other subscribers, according to circumstances, "the committee
will not accept of such, and shall intimate the same to the person or persons offering such trifling or unequal subscription,
that, unless they subscribe a sum to be named by the committee,
they shall not have any right to the use of the vault".

They later ruled that persons who did not subscribe enough
were to be struck from the register and their friends, when put
into the vault, should pay more than others. Four key bearers
were then appointed to look after the vault. One of these was
Rev. John Leslie. The apparently uncharitable gentlemen of
Udny offered non-subscribers another chance to pay 2s 6d in
addition to their subscription "as they had not become subscribers till they were forced". Key bearers were also threatened
with a fine when the fear of body-snatching passed, and they
neglected their duties. That happened in July 1836, and who
can really blame them?

Earlier on 23 February 1833 the regulations of the Udny
vault were adopted and these rules give an interesting insight
into the operation of similar burial vaults.

"1. Subscribers and their families to have the gratis use of the
vaults for themselves and their descendents in all time coming
except in such of their sons and daughters as are married, and
are householders on their own account at the present time, and
who have not subscribed for themselves, also the poor aged
parents of subscribers to be entitled to the use of the
vault.

"2. In every case the coffins to be made of good fir board, well
seasoned, seven eighths of an inch thick, the joints to be

ploughed, the head and foot to be checked into the sides, the whole ploughing, jointing and saw carves to be properly filled with white lead, ground in oil, and a piece of tow cloth to be plastered on the saw carves with hot pitch—the whole of the inside to be pitched and covered with strong paper—the lid and bottom to be double checked, the checks to be filled with putty or lead as above, and properly nailed, so as to make the coffin perfectly air tight. And in cases that might be deemed infectious or otherwise dangerous, the body to be enclosed in lead or tin plate, besides the wooden coffin.

"3. All those persons bringing bodies to the vault will be required to answer such questions as the committee may think necessary to put them regarding the coffin and body, also to bring a written attestation from the maker of the coffin binding himself under a penalty of £2 sterling that it is made in exact conformity to the above regulation for making the coffin; and if the above regulation for making the coffin shall be carelessly or insufficiently executed, so that any nuisance shall be proceed from them during the time they remain in the vault, the maker of any such coffin shall not only be liable in the above mentioned penalty, but it shall be in the power of the committee to prevent any coffin made by such persons being put into the vault, although employed by a subscriber.

"4. No body to be allowed to be longer than three months in the vault, and in cases that may be thought dangerous only for such a period as the committee shall think proper; but bodies may be removed at an earlier period if it is the desire of their friends; and if insufficiency shall be found in the coffin, the committee shall have power to refuse admittance until such insufficiency be remedied, or to cause the friends of the deceased to remove the body at any time such insufficiency may be found out.

"5. Those who are not subscribers may obtain the use of the vault on paying a sum not less than five shillings and not exceeding 20 shillings, at the option of the committee, for each body they may deposit in the vault, and conforming themselves to the same regulations as the subscribers. Any money that may be received on this account to be applied, in the same instance, to liquidate any debt that be upon the vault, and afterwards to complete such repairs as may be necessary. The committee shall also have power to give out the money received from non-subscribers towards enabling the poor to get coffins made agreeably to the foregoing regulations, and to permit those who are not able to pay to deposit the body of their deceased regulations in the vault gratis. Also that it shall be necessary for such poor persons as come from a distance to be put into the vault to bring a certificate of their circumstances from the session or minister of the parish, to be security to have the body removed in due time, and likewise if it appear (necessary) to the committee the friends of such persons as are to be deposited in the vault shall be obliged to deposit in the hands of the gravedigger a sum of money equal to the expense of internment, in case they shall fail to remove the body at the proper time.

"6. A committee of seven persons shall be chosen at a general meeting of the subscribers to be held annually on the first Saturday of July (whereof three shall be a quarum) also four extra managers, the said eleven persons to be a standing committee for the management of the affair of the concern, and to have power to enforce the strict observance of the regulations, and on the resignation or death of any of them the remaining members to have power to elect a person or persons in their room until next annual meeting.

"7. There shall be four key bearers, members of the committee, who must attend to open and shut the vault at all times necessary; but it will be desirable that those wishing admittance will give the key bearers at least twenty four hours previous warning—the key bearer to reside as near the church as can be got."

Seven rigid rules which had to be carried out to the letter, or so it seemed. A similar, but much smaller set of rules, were drawn up for the maintenance and care of a vault at Belhelvie on the Aberdeenshire coast, and these are displayed in the Anthropological Museum at Aberdeen's Marischal College. The graveyard at Belhelvie has two vaults, in fact, the larger of which was built in 1835 and was used latterly to house bodies of drowned sailors washed up on the nearby beach.

The vaults in some cases (as at Fintray, Aberdeenshire) were lined with sheet metal for protection against mildew. Long after the Anatomy Act, when the stone chambers had long past served their purpose, they were left to the death watch beetle. But at Marnoch in Banffshire the top floor of the two-storeyed chamber was used as a school. At Culsalmond, Aberdeenshire, the vault there rang with the laughter of children when in 1860 it became the headquarters of the parish Sunday school. But fertile imaginations conjured up a gallery of ghosties and the children refused to attend classes because of their school's past associations.

Open for business, the Culsalmond vault provided a source of income for the parish kirk. The walls were very thick and the iron doors doubly fashioned with the keys placed in the custody of four keepers, who were elected periodically. The mortuary attracted custom from as far away as Banff, Portsoy and Cullen, and, for the privilege, non-subscribers were charged 10s to 5s, depending on status, while locals paid from 3d to 1s. Coffins which leaked meant a job for the carpenter and a fine of £1 to the deceased's next of kin.

In Banffshire an old family tomb was converted into a watch-house. It was a pretty ram-shackle sort of building, and wild were the goings-on among the watchmen, and their cronies as they gambled and boozed the night away. One night the jollity came to a sudden halt when the floor of the old vault collapsed, dumping the living among the dead in the vault below. Playing cards, shattered whisky bottles, broken heads and all!

The Fintray vault was inaugurated in July 1830 after a local farmer's funeral. But his body did not rest in peace for long. It was scooped from the vault and the headless corpse was later found abandoned in a sack on the Dyce-Cothal road at Cothal.

But when table-topped graves, mort-safes and stone vaults failed to keep out the body-snatchers, the desperate living devised other methods. Tiny, squat stone houses were built at the entrance of cemeteries and manned by relatives and friends during the hours of darkness. These watch-houses commanded a clear view of the graveyard and they are still seen in old burial yards. Today they mostly serve for storing the gravedigger's tools. The windows and spy holes are bricked up, the tables and chairs which provided some comfort for the guardians have long disappeared. Smoke no longer curls from the chimneys. The fireplaces are as cold and dead as the people who once hunched over the friendly roar on a bone-chilling night.

...And Booby Traps

Early watch-houses were thatched with either heather or broom. In Aberdeenshire a medical student who was captured by watchmen was imprisoned in their watch-house. A man stood guard outside the only door and there seemed no way of escape for the prisoner before the constables arrived at first light. But the student's friends did not desert him, and returned in disguise in the wee small hours to tempt the unsuspecting guard with a jug of whisky. As they plied him with drink and good stories, their imprisoned companion burrowed his way through the flimsy roof and escaped. For the rest of the night the befuddled watchman guarded an empty room.

Not all watch-houses were squat, uninteresting-looking buildings. The graveyard at Banchory-Ternan, 17 miles from Aberdeen, boasts a two-storeyed tower, with its own alarm bell, which was tolled when danger threatened. The lower half of this once ivy-coated building is still used as a toolhouse and storeroom; the upper part proved an excellent look-out tower. The tiny window from which watch was kept can still be seen, and below this the circular aperture in the woodwork through which guards thrust a muzzle of a gun. Men kept watch in all cases, but there was a rare occasion in Aberdeenshire when the dead man's widow insisted on taking her turn.

Gunshot holes in some Scottish watch-houses and watch-towers prove that the people inside were not always aiming steadily, either because of nervousness, weariness or too much drink. At the clifftop cemetery at Cowie, on the northern fringe

of Stonehaven, Kincardineshire, six watchmen were alerted at
three o'clock one morning when the look-out spotted 'something
black', which appeared to move then stand still. After a hurried
debate they agreed to open fire with their shotguns. A heavy
thud followed the volley and the black thing vanished. The
oldest man in the party tried to perk up his colleagues: "Weel,
lads, we maun see what damage we've deen; he's maybe only
wounded." But on investigation they found, not a dying man,
but an inoffensive gravestone, toppled over and shattered. On
their way back to Cowie Village they were met by a party of
confused coastguards who had seen the flash of gunfire and
supposed it was a distress signal from a ship on the
rocks.

Watchmen were forbidden to be drunk on duty. Regulations
were drawn up by kirk sessions, and a set of rules issued at
Carmunnock Kirkyard in Lanarkshire in January 1828 warned
watchmen about having alcohol in the watch-house, and also of
leaving their posts during the night. Two men had to mount
guard at sunset and continue their watch until darkness lifted in
winter, or at sunrise in the summer months. They were not
supposed to have visitors, unless they knew the password for
that particular night. They had to remain silent, unless giving
the alarm. Damage to furniture and fittings in the watch-house
could lead to a fine. But rules were made to be broken, even in
the face of disapproval from the kirk.

A Speyside historian, Mr James Thomson, described the
watch-house at Aberlour, which he visited as a boy in the Banffshire whisky town. It looked like most other watch-houses of
the period, except Thomson recalled how the watchmen had an
armoury of muskets and claymores. On this particular visit he
noted an open Bible on the small wooden table, as well as a
bottle of whisky, a snuff mill and tobacco pipes. "Had the
staunchest teetotaller been there, he would have been sorely
tempted to fill the quaich and taste the contents of the bottle",

wrote Thomson in 1902, as he pointed out the hardships involved in keeping vigil for six weeks with little rest.

'Watching the dead' in Aberlour had its funny side, too. Like
the time parishioners mounted guard over the grave of a woman
whom they had believed to have been a witch. Two friends,
Jamie Gordon and Johnny Dustan reluctantly agreed to keep
watch, but while investigating a queer noise in the graveyard
in the middle of the night, they tangled with a dark, horned
beast. Johnny called in horror: "Save yourself, Jamie. We're in
the power o' the enemy. God give us gweed reddance." But they
managed to flee from 'Auld Nick', and the next morning reluctantly returned to the graveyard with townsfolk. Sitting on a
table-topped tombstone was the local daftie, Jock Fleming, who
hooted with laughter when he spotted the visitors, and jibed:
"Ye're a' feel the gither. Tibbies quiet enough in her lair. Here's
the beast that beat ye baith." Glowering under a nearby tombstone was Duncan Macpherson's legendary ram.

This animal lived with Macpherson and his family of nine
children, sharing their home and meals. It was kept tethered in
his cottage, and when it escaped, which was often, there was a
frenzied hue and cry throughout the neighbouring countryside.
It was said that when its Highland master said the family
prayers in Gaelic, the ill-tempered and ill-mannered beast went
berserk and left a trail of destruction until recaptured.

The watchmen in the mort-houses and towers were usually
relatives and friends of the dead person, but sometimes the
bereaved family paid for professionals to keep watch, but this
could lead to bribery between the resurrectionists and the hired
guards.

But as body-snatching increased, despite the safeguards,
ingenious and devilish devices were introduced. There was an
Edinburgh father who booby-trapped his daughter's grave with
a crude type of landmine. But landmines and other infernal
machines placed in the grave at burial were done with so much

publicity that it served as a warning to resurrectionists of the need to be on their guard, at all times.

The commonest method of booby-trapping a grave was the use of the spring gun, although these rarely hit the target on which they were trained. The regular body-snatcher was in no way deterred by the spring gun and one resurrectionist is on record as saying he lifted seven bodies out of one grave in a single night, although it was guarded by such a weapon. They would beat such traps by having a spy, possibly a woman dressed in black, who mingled unnoticed with the mourners, and noted the position of the gun and the pegs and trip wires needed to touch it off. When they struck that night the body-snatchers would have a roughly-sketched plan of the spot. They would carefully lift the gun, perhaps a blunderbuss, so as to relax the tension on the trip wires, carry it off a short distance uncocked. After lifting the body they would return the gun, now at full cock, leaving no sign that the grave had been disturbed.

Both professionals and amateurs had to learn the hard way. Tragedy dogged the footsteps of three Glasgow medical students who set off to rob a grave in Blackfriars Churchyard. One of them stumbled over the tripwire and was killed instantly. His two companions knew they would be implicated in a scandal if they left their dead friend behind so they adopted a macabre method of carrying away the body. They propped the body up between them, then tied the corpse's legs to theirs, at the ankles, placed his arms over their shoulders, and staggered through the darkened streets to their lodgings singing drunkenly. When they arrived at the lodgings they laid the corpse on the bed, and gave it out that he had committed suicide.

Trigger-happy watchmen proved a noisy and dangerous problem. In Old Aberdeen in 1809 the townsfolk complained bitterly to the magistrates about "people using firearms in the churchyard at night, when watching the bodies of their deceased friends, whereby danger and inconvenience may arise". Notices forbidding such practices were posted at graveyards at St Machar's Cathedral and the Spittal, also known as St Peter's Cemetery.

In April 1818 the wealthy praised the inventive genius of a London undertaker, Edward Lillie Bridgman, when he came up with a coffin made of wrought-iron. It appeared possible that the resurrectionists might be baffled and beaten. But although the coffin had no screws, hinges or movable parts and could not be opened from outside, it had an obvious drawback. His coffins were imperishable, and immediately there was a public outcry from ministers and churchwardens that the iron coffins would prevent future use of cemeteries.

But the outcry did not seem to worry Mr Bridgman and, by the following year, he claimed to have buried 100 people in fifty-two graveyards in London in his patent coffin. But the opposition to his invention steadily grew stronger, until one of his clients, a Mr Gilbert of Holburn, agreed to have his wife's interment become the subject of a test case.

Mr Gilbert brought a case against the rector of St Andrew's, Holburn, when he refused to allow his wife to be buried in an iron coffin in the burial ground at Gray's Inn Lane. Mr Bridgman made a direct appeal to the Bishop of London, who suggested that Mrs Gilbert's body should be transferred to a wooden coffin. He hinted he might be able to make the parish authorities change their mind, if the inventor undertook not to bring any more of his iron coffins for burial until after the test case had been heard in Doctor's Commons. Bridgman gleefully pointed out that once the body had been deposited in his coffin it could not be removed; the coffin was impregnable. Three months later; and Mrs Gilbert was still unburied. Even when the rector of St Andrew's died, the Bishop of London still refused to budge. It was left to the intrepid Mr Bridgman to make the next move. On 10 June 1819, Mrs Gilbert's funeral cortege arrived at the gates of the Gray's Inn burial ground. The sexton furiously slammed the gates shut in Mr Bridgman's face. After a curious mob gathered, the cortege moved on to the church itself and dumped the coffin near the front door.

At eight o'clock the sexton sent for reinforcements, and the churchwarden, the vestry clerk and several others arrived. But Bridgman refused to budge. Instead he produced a model of his invention and started to deliver a lecture. When he claimed the sexton disliked his patent because it would mean the end of bribes from body-snatchers, the night-watch were summoned. But tempers were frayed, and after a brief, bloody struggle, Mr Bridgman was hauled off to jail. When he appeared before a judge at the Guildhall the next day, Mrs Gilbert, in her iron coffin, was removed to the parish charnel house.

In September Bridgman came up for trial at the London Sessions and was acquitted. Mrs Gilbert was still unburied. But in November the patient Mr Gilbert won his case against the churchwardens of St Andrew's when Sir William Scott of the Consistory Court ruled that iron coffins were perfectly proper. At the same time he suggested that the cost of each coffin—£31 10s—should be increased.

Cock-a-hoop, Bridgman immediately placed an advertisement in newspapers, complete with an illustration of his patent. He warned that "many hundred dead bodies will be dragged from their wooden coffins this winter, for the anatomical lectures (which have just commenced), the articulators, and for those who deal in the dead for the supply of the country practitioner and the Scotch schools. The question of the right to inter in iron is now decided.

"Those undertakers who have IRON COFFINS must divide the profits of the funeral with EDWARD LILLIE BRIDGMAN. TEN GUINEAS reward will be paid on the conviction of any parish officer demanding an extra fee, whereby I shall lose the sale of a coffin. The violation of the sancity of the grave is said to be needful, for the instruction of the medical pupil, but let each one about to inter a mother, husband, child or friend, say shall I devote this object of my affection to such a purpose; if not, the only safe coffin is Bridgman's PATENT WROUGHT-IRON ONE, charged the same price as a wooden one, and is a superior substitute for lead."

Bridgman boasts that he "performs funerals in any part of the Kingdom, and by attention to moderate charges insures the recommendation of those who employ him. Twenty-five private grounds within the Bills of Mortality receive them; dues from 7s to 21s. Patent cast-iron tombs and tablets, superior to stone."

But parish officials still shunned Bridgman's iron coffins despite the triumphant tones of his advertisements. But he never missed a chance to sound his trumpet and if the theft of a body be discovered in a particular town or parish he was sure to buy space in the local newsheet to jog memories about the advantages of his invention.

More than a century after the Anatomy Act there was a serious threat to the wrought-iron mort-safes and such like. During the Second World War there was a great clamour from the Government for scrap iron and, in a nation-wide sweep, mountains of metal were collected; growing piles of everything from pots and pans to railings and old Rolls Royces.

In North-east Scotland the men from the ministry made a bid to carry off the mort-cages from several kirkyards and cemeteries. Because of the protest by local councillors and historians it was decided to leave the precious metal alone. But perhaps they would have got all the iron they required if they had gone prospecting for Mr Bridgman's patent coffins, which, if we are to believe his boasts, clutter many of London's old cemeteries.

A Letter from London

In the year of the French Revolution, six London doctors, who were also founders of the Aberdeen Medico-Chirurgical Society, sent a long letter of fatherly advice to the medical men in the northern city. It was a letter which caused a much-less bloodier revolution than the one which was tearing France apart, but the result was just as revolutionary in medical circles in North-east Scotland.

Five years before, an enthusiastic student, James McGrigor, who later became the Director-General of the Army Medical Services, formed the society with the aid of fellow medical students. Because of the deterioration in facilities for teaching anatomy at both King's and Marischal Colleges the society was welcomed by the eager students. But the society was shackled with the same problem which had faced Professor William Gordon more than 150 years before: a shortage of human specimens. They still received corpses by courtesy of the hangman and the poor house beadle.

And, like the university's first mediciner, they had to be satisfied with dead dogs. Four months after the society was orginated in 1789 the carefully-kept minute book stated: "That week a plan for anatomical dissection was put in execution. A dog was dissected. . . ." At this same meeting the students agreed to hold weekly osteological demonstrations, and arranged that each member should take his turn in lecturing.

Times were hard, and the university, too, suffered because of the dearth of 'subjects'. One early chronicler recorded, ". . . we are ashamed to say there has been no dissection, even of a dog, in the university for two years . . .". At surgeons' hall the members carried on despite the handicap; studying osteology, angiology, neurology and splanchnology, and, until 1792, they kept their resolution to dissect a dog almost every week.

But the young students desperately needed more bodies on which to practice. But from where? In April 1794, they were pointed in the direction by James McGrigor and his five colleagues.

After meeting together in London the doctors, who were still extraordinary members of the Society, dropped the bombshell. In their letter the following significant paragraph appears: "Above all we would commend to the Society the study of anatomy. We are sorry that dissections have been so long neglected at Aberdeen. We are certain that proper subjects might be easily had there, and will certainly be had, unless the students are wanting to themselves in spirited exertion or in common prudence. Bodies are procured in London for dissection almost every day. We leave anyone to form their opinion whether it would not be an easier affair at Aberdeen."

The message was loud and clear, and, although it spurred the enthusiasm of the Aberdeen medicos, it did not lead in the beginning to an outbreak of body-snatching in the area. In March 1797 a letter from a former member reads: "I am persuaded that a subject now and then might be procured at Aberdeen, and much knowledge might be acquired if the inspection of bodies at the hospital was more attended to."

The first clear reference to body-snatching in Aberdeen appears in the records of the Medico-Chirurgical Society. It appears in the well-thumbed minute book under April 29, 1800. And from this date until the end of the resurrectionist era, more than thirty years later, the practice is frequently mentioned.

In 1800 the Society cracked down on a student called Milne and a colleague for digging up a body after it had been dissected. Milne was allowed to resign on threat of expulsion and his companion, Nimmo, was fined half-a-guinea and reprimanded in front of his brethren by the president of the society. The minute records: "This disparity of punishment is owing to their former characters, Mr Milne having on several occasions divulged the secrets of the Society, particularly by informing Mr Hector's servant maids of the transactions at time of dissections, whereas Mr Nimmo had previously behaved himself in a manner compatible with the duty of a member."

In January 1801 'things' were well in hand, as a minute shows: "There was no meeting this evening as there is at present a subject under dissection." But later that year the authorities caught the first sniff of scandal, when it was discovered from where some of the bodies were coming.

A student, Charles Jameson, was charged with, having along with unnamed accomplices, stolen the body of James Marr, a miller of the Mill of Auchinbady, from its grave in the Spittal Churchyard. His father had to pay a £50 bond so that his son would keep out of trouble in the future. If not he would forfeit the money and his son would be brought back to stand trial for body-snatching.

This case is not recorded in the minutes, which is not really surprising. Jameson was the current secretary of the Society! He was appointed to the post in October 1801, twelve days before he committed the offence.

The enthusiasm of the Aberdeen students fluctuated during the next few years, as the risks involved in body-snatching became greater, and public opinion hardened against the students. The minute of November 12, 1805: "Messrs Officer, Davidson, J. Gordon and Rankine intimated to the members that they had procured a subject from the Old Town Churchyard and which was safely lodged in the anatomical theatre. Dr Skene was to take the trouble of undertaking the dissection. It is hoped that the exertions of the above will prove a stimulus to the rest of the members."

A fortnight later we read: "Messrs Forrest, Williamson, Allan and Tyrrell, on the evening of November 25, having formed a party succeeded in procuring a female subject from the New Town Churchyard and lodged it in Dr Skene's class, where the dissection is now going on."

But three months later, in February 1806, the Society was badly shaken by a scandal which had near disastrous results. The minute of February 23 states simply: "Some of the members having procured a subject lodged it in the Society's Hall, where in the course of the same day it was unfortunately discovered. At night the body was returned to the Spittal burial ground, from which it had been taken."

Next day, at an extraordinary meeting called by the president, it was announced that Sheriff Dauney had warned the Society he wanted to see the offending students. At the same time the members were informed they faced eviction from their hall. The reason was because they had used the hall for a purpose not specified in the grant. Therefore the landlord, Dr Livingston, the Society's honorary president, had decided to recall the grant. As they called the crisis meeting, Livingston had successfully applied for a warrant from the sheriff. But at the same time, the doctor had informed his worried colleagues he would willingly subscribe to the erection of a new hall.

The Society then gave their treasurer permission to "present the officers, who had discovered the body, with a small gratuity for their genteel behaviour on the occasion". The following day the four students who had taken part in the raid on the Spittal burial ground, Messrs Allan, Paterson, Rankine and J. Gordon (we have already heard of the last three named in previous entries) were examined by Sheriff Dauney in the procurator fiscal's house. The relatives and acquaintances of the dead person were advised not to go ahead with plans to prosecute the resurrectionists on account of the trouble and expense, and the president, James Allan, then penned this touching and cleverly-worded letter to the Sheriff:

"Sir, The Medical Society of Aberdeen, considering the state of the business on which some of its members were lately called before you, so disagreeable to all parties, and wishing, as far as in their power to put an end to it by any necessary concession, are willing to place their hopes of adjustment entirely in you and trust that from liberality of sentiment and your wish for the advancement of science, you may be induced to view with as much lenity as the nature of the case will permit, a fault which had for its object an improvement in one of the most important branches of medical knowledge. At the same time we assure you that we intended, after having satisfied ourselves, to have laid the body decently in the earth. We cannot but be perfectly sensible of the justice of the measures already taken, and are convinced that they might have been much more rigorous. Every person of common humanity must feel, and we, in particular, who have been the cause, do feel for the friends upon so distressing an occasion. We will, therefore, most willingly consent to defray the expenses of the re-interment, and also to submit to whatever fine you may think it proper to impose."

At a later meeting of the Society a letter was read from Sheriff Dauney signifying 'in mild terms' his disapprobation of their conduct and imposing a small fine, and at the same time submitting a note from the procurator fiscal dispensing with payment of the fine the sheriff had imposed. The minute reads: "The Sheriff wrote that the woman, whose husband had been taken up, had called on him and told him that his brothers had concealed from her the manner in which the matter had been made up and that she thought some money had been given. 'To stop her clamour' he advised that the guinea of a fine which Mr Burnett, the procurator fiscal, had not exacted should be given her. Of this all the members except three agreed to contribute their part."

In the years following medical students who were brought before the courts did not get off so lightly. In 1813 three of them from Aberdeen were caught red-handed at Banchory-Devenick, and, after a 'stiff tussle' with watchmen, they were taken to Stonehaven, where the sheriff fined them each £20 for attempting to steal a body and assault. The procurator fiscal generously handed over most of the fine to the minister at Banchory-Devenick to help the parish poor.

Two years later the courts were giving out stiffer penalties. A medical student named John Campbell was fined £100 and jailed for fourteen days at Aberdeen for robbing a grave. In 1817, three young apprentice surgeons from Keith, Banffshire, were each jailed for four months. They were employed by John Gordon, the surgeon at Keith, and were arrested after 'snatching' the body of one John Bremner, who had been interred in the town cemetery. They were dealt with by the Spring Circuit Court in Aberdeen. By 1826, the sentences did not seem as harsh. Student Alexander Matthew was fined £20 and imprisoned for a month for taking up a body at Inverurie.

After the Aberdeen Medico-Chirurgical Society had been expelled from Dr Livingston's property they removed their library, museum and meeting place to Dr Skene's classroom in Marischal College in 1806. They later occupied houses in North Street and Longacre, before they became established in their new, handsome hall in King Street in 1820. But Dr Livingston continued to help the Society. He was after all their first honorary president, and he had been appointed professor of medicine of the University in 1793.

The Society's cherished minutes record little of interest in 1807, except to note that it cost 11s for two pints of whisky to top up specimen bottles.

But in 1808, the year Mrs Spark's body vanished mysteriously from St Fittick's Churchyard, the members had to deal with problems of a far more domestic nature. It seems some students were indiscreet and divulged information about post-mortems and body-snatching to outsiders. And three members attempted to steal a corpse from the Society's meeting rooms! A minute solemnly states: "It seems they had endeavoured to remove it on Monday night but were not able to accomplish their object, but intended to have made another trial this evening with one person more to assist them."

The body was eventually found in another room in the building, and their lack of counter body-snatching pleased no one, for the records state that the other members "would certainly have been much obliged to them (for stealing the body) as no one would endanger themselves by lecturing on the joints or muscles or even cleaning the bones, the subject was so far advanced in the putrefactive fermentation".

After a serious leakage of information in the same year, it was unanimously carried: "That if any member be convicted of intentionally giving information of any subject the Society may procure for dissection, he shall *ipso facto* be expelled." The ruling was rushed through after a member of the public, a man called Sheriffs, had publicly given information and details of a body-snatching expedition in St Nicholas Kirkyard.

𝕾𝖍𝖔𝖙𝖙𝖞 𝖆𝖓𝖉 𝕺𝖙𝖍𝖊𝖗𝖘

—

'Shotty' Ross was a strange freak of nature. He had a tough, muscular body of normal size and length but his legs were short and bowed, out of all proportion to the rest of his frame. But despite the physical handicap, 'Shotty', christian name Alexander, carried on a tailor's business in the parish of Drumoak in West Aberdeenshire. He also had a wonderful self-conceit and overmastering sense of self-importance. But for all that he was a well kent and well-liked character in that part of Lower Deeside.

One of Shotty's friends was a giant of a man, the bearded blacksmith Charles Edward, who had the smiddy at Peterculter, a few miles east of Drumoak. But, despite his bulk, he could be gentle as the lambs which gambolled in the fields outside his smiddy, but, when roused, his temper would flare like his forge.

When 'Shotty' died, rumours swept the parishes of Drumoak and Peterculter that attempts would certainly be made by resurrectionists to lift his deformed body. On the night after 'Shotty' was buried in Dalmaik Kirkyard a farmer who lived on the border of the two parishes saw six men making their way westwards by horse and gig. He suspected they were medical students. About an hour or so later he saw the gig return from the direction of the kirkyard, so he mounted his horse and rode off to blurt out his suspicions to the blacksmith.

He gave his horse to Charles Edward, who set off in hot pursuit; hair, beard and leather apron flying. When he overtook the body-snatchers at the Stonegavel Inn on the outskirts of Peterculter four of the men were walking in the rear of the gig.

He pulled the sweating horse up in a flurry of dirt and thundered at the strangers: "What have you got in that sack?" The strange garb of the man on horseback, and the expression of rage on his smoke-blackened and sweat-streaked face no doubt gave the body-snatchers the notion that the smith had come from warmer quarters than the smiddy at Culter.

At the sight of the blacksmith, the six men fled into a nearby wood, leaving behind the horse, gig, and sack. The 'smith ripped open the sack with a clasp knife and out popped his late friend's bald head. He then drove back to Drumoak in the gig, with the farmer's horse tethered to it.

A triumphant crowd cheered the strange procession on the journey back to Dalmaik Kirkyard, where 'Shotty' was put back in his coffin. They never did trace his resurrectionists, but a few days later the horse and gig were claimed by a horse-hirer from Aberdeen.

Today 'Shotty' sleeps peacefully in an unmarked grave near other members of the Ross clan in the tiny kirkyard of Dalmaik, which nestles in a remote spot on the banks of the River Dee. The bell in the belfry has not summoned a congregation since 1836. The kirk and nearby manse have proved less durable than a cast iron 'tombstone' which has been propped against the south wall of the kirk, which has roots stretching back to 1062.

The farming folk of Dalmaik had a sense of humour, if the epitaph of one of their community of 1809 is anything to judge by:

> In Carnie sure did Davie die,
> We hope his soul's in heaven high.
> The body lies beneath this stone,
> To moulder here both skin and bone.
> It was his blessed will to wear,
> A coat without a seam,
> Which fitted well in every part,
> Wove in a wyver's leem.

Unfortunately, their minister did not see the funny side of this strange epitaph and ordered the last four lines to be chiselled out!

Of course, if Shotty's resurrectionists had been patient they could have plucked up enough courage to return for the dwarf's skeleton. Perhaps they did. Medical schools coveted such skeletons. One of England's greatest surgeons, John Hunter, hired men to watch the home of the Irish circus giant, Charles Byrne, when he was tipped off that he was dying. Byrne, who was seven feet six inches in height, once amazed the citizens of Edinburgh by lighting his pipe at their streetlamps. Byrne knew his body would be prized by the anatomists and pleaded with his dying breath that his corpse be watched day and night, until he was buried at sea in a lead coffin. But Hunter bribed the watchmen and the giant corpse was carried to his house in Earl's Court, where it was boiled so that only the skeleton was left.

One of Sir Walter Scott's characters, the 'Black Dwarf', David Ritchie in real life, had a horror of being dissected. But in 1821, ten years after he was buried at Manor, near Peebles, curious doctors from Glasgow resurrected his bones. 'Bowed Davie' loved poetry and quoted Milton and Shakespeare, but the prayer on his tombstone was disregarded:

> Good friend! For Jesus' sake forbear
> To dig the dust enclosed here;
> Blest be the man that spares these stones,
> And curst be he that moves my bones.

If 'Shotty Ross' was allowed to rest in peace, one of his neighbours was not so lucky. The parishioners, suspicious that a woman's grave had been robbed, visited Dalmaik Cemetery with her husband. As they dug down to the coffin he watched silently from a few yards away, his chin resting on his staff. Suddenly there was a shout from one of the exhumers, "John, she's nae here!" The husband, so it is said, lifted his head wearily and spoke: "Fent a stime o' her see I, but ae thing I ken, an' that is that I put her into the grun since; but they'll look wi' clear e'en that'll see me pit her in again."

Students who went in search of 'things' for their surgeon faced great risks to life and limb if caught. On their midnight rambles they found Dutch courage in a dram or two of whisky.

In Aberdeenshire, as in the rest of Scotland, the body-snatchers were feared and despised and their work was regarded as a gruesome interference with a Scotsman's chance of enjoying the life hereafter. When a person died the custom in North-east Scotland was to place lighted candles beside the corpse. Then a saucer of unmixed salt and earth was laid on its breast; the earth as emblematical of the corruptible body and salt symbolical of the immortal spirit. All the clocks in the house were stopped at the time of death and not re-started until after the funeral.

Certain parishes observed an interesting custom by using mortcloths to cover the coffin from the time the corpse was placed in the coffin until burial. The mortcloth was usually a large, black velvet cloth, ornamented with white, and was hired out by the kirk session. In Gartly, Aberdeenshire, locals paid 2s 6d, while people from outside the parish were charged 3s.

The custom originates through an ancient Highland superstition that a murderer would escape eternal justice if he could see below his victim's coffin. That's why a plaid or flag draped over the coffin reached the ground. Highland folklore tells of murderers who were caught red-handed trying to steal a 'keek' below the plaid. Some parishes had a small mortcloth for children. A well preserved mortcloth is in the safe-keeping of Peterculter Parish Church.

Deeside, the valley of British Kings and Queens, proved a happy hunting ground for the Aberdeen resurrectionists, and a number of watch-houses were built. But the medical students cast a wide net and even the graveyard at Marnoch, in the upper reaches of Banffshire, was not out of reach for the raiding parties. This remote parish was the centre of one amusing legend. After the body-snatchers had lifted the coffin from the grave, they heard approaching voices, and quickly darted behind the tombstones. At that moment two farmhands looked over the wall and saw the corpse hanging half out of the coffin. Suspecting the students would return to collect the body, one of the locals switched the body for himself, and settled down to wait for the fun to start. When the students sneaked back one of them whispered to his companions: "C'mon boys, give me a hand with him." Back came the voice from the coffin: "Let be, lads, I'll rise mysel'." Exit the students, empty-handed and in great haste!

Night raids on Royal Deeside were sometimes just as unrewarding. The kirkyard of Banchory-Devenick, which stands at the foot of a sloping hill only a few yards from the River Dee and takes its name from St Devenick, was frequently visited by the Aberdeen medical school. In 1807, after a little boy had died at Aberdeen Infirmary, a raiding party was organised. The university lecturer had hinted to the students that it was desirable the boy should be buried in the kirkyard, "in order that it might be found out what was the matter with him".

The boy was eventually buried at Banchory-Devenick and a few nights later a band of medical students set out on a frosty moonlight night for the churchyard, less than two miles from the old Bridge of Dee, on the Kincardineshire bank. Safely arrived they quickly began digging. But their wooden spades splintered on the frozen surface. They next forced open the sacristy door, then used the pewter 'bawbee' ladles, used for Sabbath collections, to unearth the tiny coffin. The sack was filled and handed to a student, nicknamed 'Long Ned', and the procession returned to Aberdeen on foot.

As they hurried along the road, they became aware of angry

voices at their rear and immediately quickened their step. They soon reached the old brig with its seven arches, and were half-way across when they were confronted by a gang of men charging angrily towards them from the Aberdeen side. Turning to fly, they were faced with their pursuers from Banchory-Devenick, who had discovered what they had done.

Trapped in the centre of the bridge, the students urgently advised 'Long Ned' to dump the sack into an ice hole beneath the bridge, so that it might be retrieved when the coast was clear. But Long Ned's aim was unsteady and the bundle splashed into the river, twenty feet below. The sack bobbed in the icy current and was swept within a few feet of the northern bank where it was scooped up by the boy's relatives, who had recruited the band of rescuers after their suspicions had been aroused in Aberdeen. Fists and feet flew as the students struggled with their attackers on the brig, but somehow they managed to escape. One of the Medico-Chirurgical Society's members who had played a prominent part in the raid later became a leading doctor in Aberdeen. But the day after the Banchory-Devenick fiasco he discreetly went into 'hiding', by going to stay with his uncle in Peterhead for three weeks or so.

The Aberdeen students did not bring the 'things' directly back to the Marischal College or medical school for dissection. To carry a sack on a gig or one's back after dark would have invited investigation by the town guard. Instead the body-snatchers would conceal the body in empty houses or ruins to be carried off the next day by a porter.

Old buildings suddenly took on a reputation of being haunted. In Mary Place, Aberdeen, there was such a house, where superstitious neighbours were kept away by stories of strange figures in white which flitted at the windows and in and out of doors. The 'ghost' was later laid by a couple. It was a medical student in disguise and they were friendly with his family. The house in Mary Place was a former villa which had a door on either side which suited the purpose of the students as it proved an excellent short-cut to Old Aberdeen.

At Bieldside, a hamlet five miles from Aberdeen, a minister's man found a body stolen from a Deeside kirkyard and dumped in his master's summer house. And one young Aberdeen student was said to have ruined his father's business by hiding a body in a flour sack in the baker's house.

It was not always students disguised in shrouds who handed out the shocks. Sometimes it worked the other way round. Two watchmen guarding the tomb of a former member of an influential Aberdeen family fled from Aberdeen's 'Mither Kirk'—St Nicholas Churchyard—when a woman in white flitted noiselessly through the tombstones towards them. She, in fact, had not seen them. The woman lived nearby and had gone for a moonlight walk in her stocking feet. She explained her story to the men, when they eventually plucked up courage to return to the graveyard.

At Cowie Kirkyard a student bolted after hearing groans. They came from a tinker curled up under a tombstone for the night.

Some body-snatchers decided the best way to transport their 'subjects' back to the anatomical theatre should be simple and straightforward. At Edrom, a hamlet in the Scottish Borders, a Duns publican and his friend were driving home from Gifford Fair when they saw three figures in an approaching gig. Two of the men lost their nerve and leapt clear, but the third remained bolt upright. He was a corpse of a man called McGall, buried the day before at Edrom. A culvert a mile from the hamlet where his coffin was found is still known as McGall's Brig. An Allantown woman, Mary Manuel, who dressed McGall for his first funeral, had to dress him for his second.

Glasgow students risked detection at the city's toll gates when returning from an outing in the country. Two resourceful students found a way round the problem when they drove out to rob a cemetery at Mearns in south-east Renfrewshire. They took a suit of old clothes with them and, after getting their body, they dressed it up. They sat the dead man between them in the chaise and got past the Gorbals toll-keeper by pretending they were taking a very drunk friend home. As they jogged away the tollkeeper shouted: "O, puir auld bodie, he looks unco' ill in the face; drive cannily hame, lads; drive cannily."

Aberdeen, too, had its enterprising body-snatchers. A Professor in Medicine at the Marischal College was said to have regularly driven into the quadrangle with a fresh corpse in his passenger seat. On one occasion the mob thronged outside the college gate after it was rumoured he had been seen with a strange-looking woman passenger. Police soon dispersed the crowd.

During the winter, when the country roads were choked by snowdrifts, the Aberdeen students would sometimes set off in hired boats up the River Dee on lightning raids on graveyards. Banchory-Devenick, Peterculter, Dalmaik and Banchory-Ternan were ideally situated for this purpose.

A group of Aberdeen medical students rowed the eight twisting miles to Peterculter to lift a body. Their deed was executed more for its daring nature, than in the cause of science, and was known to only a few outside their faculty. The reason? It happened fifty years after the Anatomy Act, when the fear and revulsion of body-snatching had vanished!

Grim Tales of Two Cities

Before the Burke and Hare horrors, Edinburgh was shocked by the sinister activities of four weird body-snatchers called Merry Andrew, Moudiewarp (The Mole), Spune and Praying Howard. When they were not trying to swindle each other, they proved a highly-efficient team.

Merry Andrew, real name Andrew Merrilees, was the ringleader. He was a long, thin creature with scraggy, ill-fitting clothes who jerked like a puppet as he walked, his gaunt face twitching repeatedly. He began life as a carter with a thirst for whisky, drinking a bottle a day. So when he ran short of money he turned to body-snatching, which was not too difficult as his house outside Edinburgh adjoined a graveyard. But when whisky loosened his tongue he had to leave the neighbourhood in a hurry.

Spune was given his nickname because of his knack in scooping bodies from their coffins. He was a short, sober-faced man in long, greasy black clothes. He was also a deaf mute. The Mole, whose name was Mowatt, did most of the digging. This left Praying Howard, whose job it was to attend pauper's funerals, say a few prayers, offer some words of comfort to the bereaved, then rush away to tip-off the gang about a suitable subject.

It suited Merry Andrew and his cronies to get a specimen without too much back-breaking. But one evening the tables were turned on Merry Andrew, who was a frequent target for the fun-loving students of old Edinburgh. He was spotted loitering at the mouth of a close in the Canongate by a student, who decided to play an instant prank on the resurrectionist. Guessing Andrew was waiting for a message from someone living in the evil-smelling close, the student tip-toed up to him, whispered, "She's dead", and then vanished.

Merry Andrew hurried into the house at the end of the close where a prospective 'subject' lay dying. He threw open the door of the hovel and bawled at the old woman sitting at the bedside: "It's a' owre, I hear," he said. "And when wull we come for the wummun's corp'?" The old croan glared at the lanky intruder and told him to clear off. But Merry Andrew refused to believe that the woman in the bed was still clinging to life. He bent his gaunt, ghastly features over the sick woman, then, rushed outside to try and catch the hoaxer.

The old woman died the following night as Merry Andrew and his gang returned to the house to claim the body. They carried a sack filled with tanner's bark, which would be substituted for the corpse. But the woman who was sitting up with the body had a change of heart about parting with the corpse. Perhaps the price was not right. Anyway, she refused to allow the body-snatchers to take away the body. Merry Andrew, undaunted, sent out for a bottle of whisky from a nearby spirit dealer's shop, while he tried to talk the woman out of her stubborness. The whisky worked wonders. After a few drams and a payment of three pounds, Merry Andrew was given permission to unscrew the coffin lid.

But at that precise moment there was a sharp rap at the door. The woman opened it to a young man, who asked to see the body as he was the dead woman's nephew. The body-snatchers excused themselves before scurrying off into the darkness. They had broken no laws, but, at first, they were too jittery to return to the flat to recover the three pounds and sack. When they did pluck up courage, they learned they had been hoaxed. The nephew was another student, who, in the interval, had clinched a deal with the croan, and carried the corpse off to his apartments.

The Mole and Spune had less success at trying to cheat their leader. Merry Andrew had an elder sister living at Penicuik on the outskirts of Edinburgh. She became seriously ill and one day they spotted Merry Andrew wearing black. They put their heads together and decided to reach St Mungo's Cemetery at Penicuik before their leader, and steal Miss Merrilees' body.

Mole borrowed a pedlar's cart and that night he and Spune journeyed to Penicuik. They were in luck and found the graveyard unguarded. They quickly unearthed the late Miss Merrilees and were about to pop her into the sack when they heard an uncanny noise from behind a tombstone. They slowly turned their heads; then froze in horror as a ghastly apparition in a white shroud jumped into the air with a wild shriek. The terror-struck resurrectionists clawed and stumbled towards the cemetery wall, fearful the 'thing' would chase them. But Merry Andrew had no intention of wasting his energy on his terrified cronies. He had gone to the graveyard after his suspicions had been aroused when told the pair had hired a cart, without taking him into their confidence.

He had dressed in the shroud to give them the fright of their miserable lives. Afterwards he pulled his sister's body from her coffin and stuffed her into the sack his loyal friends had dropped. He then drove back to Edinburgh to sell the body to the surgeons.

Edinburgh's rival city, Glasgow, never had a medical school large enough to employ professional body-snatchers, so students and lecturers went foraging for bodies by themselves. But the body-snatching fear gripped Glaswegians and country folk just the same, and clubs were formed to protect cemeteries.

In Glasgow the North Quarter Friendly Churchyard Guard Association was formed to protect the High Churchyard and it boasted of 2,000 members. Students on the prowl had to keep a sharp look-out for the city's early police force and night watch-men, dubbed 'Charlies', who carried lanterns and rattles and had a sentry box in which to take shelter. But the 'Charlies', usually elderly Highlanders, had a worrying enough problem to deal with in Glasgow's unlit streets—the local Hell Fire Club. These young hell-raisers rode through the streets wearing white hoods, like the Ku Klux Klan, and with the hooves of their horses muffled. They went in search of citizens to terrify or a Charlie to imprison like an outraged tortoise under his tipped sentry box.

Rumblings against the city's medical students began in the 18th century and in 1803 the university had to retain a party of soldiers for their protection against an angry mob. But the full vent of this anti-student feeling boiled over in December 1813 when two funerals took place on the same day; the thir-teenth. One was the burial of Mrs McAlister, the wife of a Hutchison Street haberdasher, in the Ramshorn Cemetery, and the other in the Cathedral churchyard. The students divided their forces. The Cathedral raiders returned unmolested to the medical school with two corpses, one more than they had set out to capture.

The Ramshorn party dug up Mrs McAlister but were later spotted by a patrolling constable. The next morning angry rela-tives and a mob of citizens marched on the chief constable's house. And when it was discovered that Mrs McAlister's grave was empty, their fury was directed on the surgeons and in par-ticular on the home of the professor of anatomy at Glasgow University, Dr James Jeffrey. Before the mob was dispersed they had smashed every single window in the doctor's house.

The magistrates, concerned that the mob might go berserk, immediately issued search warrants authorising the police to enter, by force if necessary, any premises they thought might conceal Mrs McAlister's body. Relatives and friends of the dead woman and her surgeon-dentist, James Alexander, who had attended her on the day of her death, accompanied the police in the hunt.

They concentrated their search in the High Street and Ingram Street area and one of the first premises they searched was the dissecting rooms of Dr Granville Sharp Pattison, the newly-appointed lecturer in anatomy at the University. They were in-invited by Pattison to comb the College Street building thoroughly and, after a detailed hunt, they found nothing and left. But the dentist recalled seeing a tub of discoloured water which had not been investigated, and the searchers returned to the rooms.

At the bottom of the tub they found a human jawbone and other parts of a body including some fingers. The dentist was able to identify the jawbone and others identified Mrs McAlister's wedding ring. Dr Pattison and his lecturer and students were arrested, then stoned by the crowd as they were dragged off to jail. Later as they reflected on their escape from lynching, police found the remains of several bodies concealed under the floorboards in College Street.

On June 6, 1814, Pattison, his lecturer, Andrew Russell, and two students, Robert Munro and John McLean, appeared on indictment at the High Court of Justiciary at Edinburgh, charged with "ruthlessly and feloniously" violating Mrs McAlister's grave and taking her body to the dissecting rooms "where it was found and identified". The defence counsel asked for the trial to be held in camera, but this was refused by the court, which ruled that it could be granted only in cases of "adultery and the like". But it was an open and shut case. Pattison's counsel concentrated on the question of identification, and succeded in showing that, although Mrs McAlister had been a wife and mother, a "significant part of the body was from a virgin". What the police search party had done was complete a macabre jig-saw of the portions of bodies found in Pattison's rooms.

All four accused were acquitted, but because of the stigma following the case, and a scandal involving a doctor's wife, Pattison emigrated to America. Nearly twenty years later he gave evidence to the Warburton Select Committee, and seemed unrepentant over the McAlister case when he replied to their questions.

Question: "In your time in what manner did the police or magistrates treat the practice of exhumation; were they vigilant in their endeavours to prevent or detect the commission of the offence, zealous to expose it to the public eye when detected, and severe in punishing it upon conviction; or, on the contrary, were they disposed to tolerate and overlook the offence as being, under the existing laws on the subject, an unavoidable and necessary evil?"

Pattison: "On the contrary, they behaved with the greatest severity; in my own individual case, the first year I taught there was a body disinterred, and there was a skull without teeth found in my dissecting rooms, and because this person had had no teeth, I was dragged away by the police, carried through the populace, pelted with stones; I was then indicted, and tried like a common criminal in Edinburgh, a man sitting on each side of me with a drawn bayonet."

"What was the result of the trial? An acquittal, which cost me £520." He did not tell the eminent gentlemen that his students had been given keys to deposit bodies in his lecture rooms at any hour of night.

Pattison was a fiery and controversial figure, who inevitably became involved in a number of public scandals in Scotland, and later in the United States. He was the youngest son of John Pattison of Kelvingrove and after his education at the High School of Glasgow, and at University, he became an assistant in the College Street School of Anatomy in 1809. The master anatomist of this private school was Allan Burns, on whose death at an early age was succeeded by Pattison. In 1813, the doctor was admitted qua surgeon to the Faculty of Physicians and Surgeons of Glasgow, and three years later he was appointed surgeon to Glasgow Royal Infirmary. But his quick-fire temper led him to his first major quarrel. A Director of the Infirmary, Hugh Miller, accused him of unprofessional conduct at a consultation in the hospital. The surgeon demanded an inquiry by the management, which included Miller, but he was found in the wrong and reprimanded.

By 1818, Pattison was Professor of Anatomy at the Andersonian University, an institution founded in 1796 by John Anderson, known to everyone as 'Jolly Jack Phosphorus'. 'Jolly Jack' was Professor of Natural Philosophy at Glasgow University, but fought with all his colleagues and when he died left estate to found a rival institution.

His dying wish was that: "The professors of this university shall not be permitted, as in some other colleges, to be drones or triflers, drunkards or negligent of their duty in any manner of way."

But Pattison did not stay long at Andersonian, for in the year 1818-19 he was named by Dr William Ure as co-respondent in a divorce case. But the Council of the Andersonian and London University cleared him after studying his papers and evidence. He moved across the Atlantic where he hoped to succeed the Professor of Anatomy at the University of Pennsylvania in Philadelphia. But the chair was filled by the time his boat docked and, after refusing an invitation to the University of Transylvania at Lexington, he set himself up as a private teacher in anatomy in Philadelphia, attracting 190 students.

In a short time he had made enemies. Word of the divorce scandal reached America and he became involved in a head-on clash with Dr Nathaniel Chapman, Professor of Theory and Medicine in the University of Pennsylvania, who had set out to ruin Pattison by mounting a one-man campaign of hate, fanned by unfounded reports and pamphlets. On October 23, 1820,

Pattison branded Chapman as a "liar, a coward and a scoundrel" and challenged him to a duel. But Pattison did not get satisfaction. He was arrested instead, but later released.

Two years later he did fight a duel. But his opponent was Chapman's brother-in-law, General Thomas Cadwallader, whom he wounded in the arm with a pistol ball.

Pattison's museum was shipped from Glasgow to the States and he promptly sold its 1,000 specimens to the University of Maryland for 8,000 dollars. In 1821 a building was erected to house the vast collection. Five years later he returned to Britain. Ill-health was given as the reason, but some said the Glaswegian had his eye on the newly-founded chair of anatomy at London University. But the Scot was not popular, and he quarrelled with Dr J. R. Bennett, who was made demonstrator of anatomy without his knowledge. Even after Bennett's death, rumours and accusations were spread about Pattison, and, even although he was appointed to the chair of surgery in 1831, he decided to go back to America.

He took over the chair of anatomy at Jefferson College, Philadelphia, and a few years later married a Scots girl, Mary Sharp. In 1840 he founded the Bellevue Medical Centre in New York. He was 60 when he died in November 1851.

Although he edited several important journals on anatomy in the United States, and during his life had filled five professorial chairs, Pattison was also deeply interested in music and the arts, and was a founder member of the Grand Opera House in New York.

Probably Glasgow's worst 'body-snatcher' riot occurred in 1822 when an inquisitive, and, as it turned out, very imaginative citizen peered through the basement windows of a gloomy mansion belonging to an oil and colour merchant named George Provand. He thought he saw rivers of blood and the severed heads of two children. He blurted out his horrible tale to all Glasgow, and soon a mob swept down Clyde Street towards the mansion, which had an evil reputation as a previous owner, Bob Dragon, had committed suicide. The mob battered down the door and proceeded to dump most of the contents of the house in the River Clyde, but the more valuable items were pocketed.

The magistrates called out the military; the cavalry from Laurieston Barracks and the infantrymen from barracks in the Gallowgate. The Riot Act was read and the crowd dispersed without bloodshed. If they had looked, they would have found that the blood in the basement was in fact red paint, and there was no trace of severed heads.

Next morning the Lord Provost of Glasgow offered a reward of 200 guineas for information leading to the arrest of the ringleaders. Five persons were tried and convicted, and one of them, Richard Campbell, became the last man to be whipped through the streets of Glasgow by the last Glasgow public hangman. Campbell had not only led the rioters but had helped himself to as much gold and silver as he could carry from the sacked mansion.

Ringed by a detachment of the 4th Dragoon Guards, Campbell was brought out of the Tolbooth jail at Glasgow Cross on May 8, 1832 and lashed to a cart. The reluctant hangman, Thomas Young, who was said to be so ashamed of his craft that he stayed indoors except when duty called, administered eighty lashes by the time the cart had dragged the bleeding and unconscious prisoner back to the jail, where he stayed until he was deported.

Not Wanted on Voyage

When the Irish sloop berthed at Glasgow docks in the high summer of 1813 its hold bulged with a cargo of bales of rags. These fat bundles were bound for a well-known huckster in Jamaica Street, but he refused to accept the bales when told the freight charges amounted to the improbable sum of £50.

The bales were unloaded on the quayside and stored in a shed in the Broomielaw. But in the next few days an evil stench swept the dockland and a complaint was lodged with the customs. When the city guard cut open the bales out tumbled the decomposing bodies of men, women, children and various bits and pieces. The huckster had never received a note from his Irish contact warning him about the grisly cargo.

Glasgow, like most British ports, was a clearing house for corpses imported from abroad. Ships carrying such cargo called at London, Liverpool, Bristol, Leith and Aberdeen. The demand for 'subjects' was never satisfied. Granville Sharp Pattison was to tell the Warburton Select Committee years after: "In Glasgow, at present, bodies are so scarce that they are salted in the summer and hung up and dried like Yarmouth herrings."

Dublin proved the hub of the export trade in bodies, with Le Havre and other Continental ports close behind. A Scottish half-pay surgeon, Wilson Rae, nicknamed 'The Captain', earned his living packaging corpses and shipping them across the Irish Sea in steamboats. The innocent-looking containers were usually labelled, 'books', 'pianos', or even 'glue', depending on the individual size and weight. But Rae and his wife, who transported the cargo by cart to the docks, were arrested after rumours swept Dublin that innocent children were murdered to keep up the horrible trade. The rumours sparked off a riot during which the porter of the College of Surgeons was killed. But the strange export business still carried on. Some corpses were sent direct to Glasgow, or via Greenock and the Forth and Clyde Canal to Edinburgh. Others went by sea to London, but because of the high risk of cargoes rotting before reaching their destination, the medical schools preferred the goods shipped to Liverpool, before being transported by road to various parts of the country.

But the route to Liverpool and beyond had many pitfalls. In October 1826, three casks were delivered to St George's Dock on Merseyside. The casks were marked, 'Bitter Salts' and were put aboard the smack *Latona*, bound for Leith, and addressed to 'Mr G. H. Ironson' of Edinburgh. But the dock labourers complained to the captain about the sickening smell and when he opened a cask he found the reason. The police had the casks removed to a dockland mortuary, where they were found to contain the bodies of four men and seven women, expertly packed in salt after having being pickled in brine. The police traced the casks to a cellar in Hope Street, Liverpool, where they found twenty-two corpses, of both sexes; young and old, packed in barrels and sacks.

Three Scotsmen were eventually brought to trial, and were given jail sentences and a fine of £50 each. Three months later a box was handed in at Dublin, addressed to a 'Mr Thomson' of Bedford Square, London, and marked 'Speed'. It was not until ten days later that the box was put aboard the steam packet *Manchester*, a few hours before it sailed. By the time the box arrived at Liverpool docks two days later it became clear why the sender had urged a speedy delivery. It contained the body of a man.

The medical student (*from an old engraving*)

PLATE 5

William Hare (*from a contemporary drawing*)

PLATE 6

William Burke (*from a contemporary drawing*)

PLATE 7

Mary Paterson: Edinburgh prostitute and victim of Burke
and Hare as interpreted by United Artists in the film *Burke
and Hare* (1972)

PLATE 8

Mary Paterson (*from a contemporary drawing in the collection of Edinburgh Corporation Library*)

Some grim scenes from the film *Burke and Hare* (*a Kenneth Shipman production distributed by United Artists*)

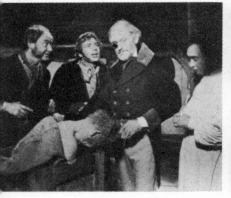

PLATE 9

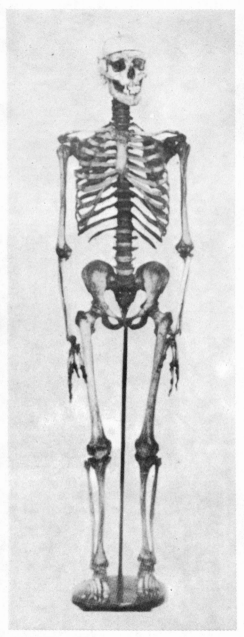

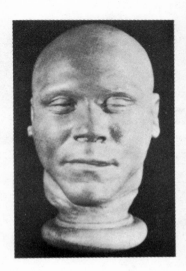

The skeleton and death-mask of
Burke preserved at Edinburgh
University Medical School

PLATE 10

The Edinburgh mob pursuing Burke's woman, Helen
McDougal (*from an old engraving*)

PLATE 11

A romanticised Victorian interpretation: The medical
student recognising the body of his dead mother

PLATE 12

Bodies were plentiful in impoverished Ireland. In Dublin the price of a corpse in the early days of body-snatching was only 10s. The Irish 'sack-'em-up-men' were sometimes helped by the friends of the dead paupers, and pubs near Bully's Acre cemetery kept picks and shovels free for needy customers who wanted to dig up the price of a pint in a hurry.

Hundreds of consignments passed through Dublin without detection, and customers were to be found in Oxford, Manchester, Birmingham, Bristol and Exeter, but the main supply line led to Scotland. The resurrectionists disguised the goods as consignments coming from drysalter, pork curers, fish mongers and even apple dealers. But faulty packing and lack of suitable deodorants caused the downfall of the careless. The Leith smack frequently found itself storm-bound, with as many as twelve bodies consigned for medical schools in Edinburgh. This inevitably led to strong complaints by passengers and the detection of the bodies, which were then buried at sea.

But with such a booming export trade it was not long before the Irish anatomists complained bitterly of the shortage of 'subjects' for their own use. The Irish Surgeon-General echoed their feelings to the Irish Secretary and pointed out in his letter that the corpse-famine had sharply increased prices.

Dr Knox of Edinburgh penned an angry letter to Sir Robert Peel, the Home Secretary. He reported that: "During the course of last summer, two cases containing anatomical subjects were shipped on board a steam packet in Dublin Harbour. A few hours previous to the sailing of the vessel, one of the lecturers in Dublin, who had probably received information of the shipment, sent his assistant on board, who, suspecting the boxes to contain subjects, procured a warrant, had them broken up and their contents left exposed on the quay, for, as I am informed, the space of two days, apparently for the purpose of irritating the populace and preventing the supply of the schools; and this at a time when subjects abounded so much in Dublin that to use a mercantile phrase, the article was in no demand whatever."

Knox never posted the letter, which also contained criticism of the Scottish medical authorities. Two days later Burke was arrested, and he had other things with which to occupy his mind.

At the height of the Irish trade a number of bodies were intercepted inland. A number of inquests were held at Carlisle on bodies being carried by the mail coaches, which stabled in the town for a night on the journey to Scotland. The verdict was almost always the same: "Found dead in a box."

The price of a 'subject' sent from London rose to £20 during one period, and any destruction to a cargo meant a great financial loss to the consignees. In one session Dr Knox was said to have been out of pocket by £800. On one occasion he sent £200 to Ireland for supplies and lost the lot.

The London body-snatcher Joseph Naples has also left details of the monstrous export trade for posterity. Sixteen pages torn from a diary he kept, during the sessions of the London anatomical schools from October to May in the years 1811 and 1812, are cherished by the Royal College of Surgeons in London.

The 'log-book', as Naples called his diary, shows that he and his fellow resurrectionists led a busy, and prosperous, life by night and day. Here, for instance, is the entry for five days in December 1812:

Tuesday, 1st: Met at Tottenham Court Road. Had a dispute in St Thomas's crib. Came home without doing anything. Went to the Rockingham Arms and got drunk.

Wednesday, 2nd: Met at Mr Vicker's pub. Rectified our last account. The party sent out me and Ben to St Thomas's Crib. Got one adult. Bill and Jack went to Guy's crib. Got two adults. Took them to St Thomas's. Came home. Met at St Thomas's. Me and Jack went to Tottenham. Got four adults. Ben and Bill went to St Pancras. Got six adults, one small and one foetus. Took the Tottenham lot to Wilson, the St Pancras lot to Bart's.

Thursday 3rd: Met at Windmill Street. Disposed of two of above to Wilson. Went to Bart's. Came home for the night.

Friday 4th: Met at Vicker's pub. Afterwards went to St Thomas's. Got six adults and took them to Bart's. Packed up one for Shute. Left Ben and Jack Hutton to pack up for Edinburgh. Afterwards Jack, me and Bill went to Tottenham. Got three adults. Took them to Bart's.

Saturday 5th. Remained at Bart's packing up for Edinburgh. Sent twelve to the wharf.

Naples and his cronies did brisk business with Edinburgh medical schools and, for a while, their prices were stabilised; four guineas for an adult, three and a half for a corpse which had been 'opened', and a guinea for a child. Of course several 'rackets' were operated by the body-snatchers, the most popular being to deliberately cut off supplies to anatomists, thus sending prices sky-high. At one time the London gangs went on strike when they did not get the prices they demanded from the medical schools. But there was always a body-snatcher willing to sell, and the price ring was soon broken.

With vast fortunes being made by English, Irish and Europeon resurrectionists, the Scots, predictably, investigated the possibilities of turning their own burial yards into a source of supply for surgeons beyond their borders.

In 1825, Joshua Brookes, proprietor of the Blenheim Street medical school in London, received a letter from a friend in the West Highlands who observed: "There are plenty of subjects to be got here in the Highlands, for there are churchyards without churches and very distant from any house. I should suppose also that from the great bodily exertions which the Highlanders are accustomed to, in climbing their mountains, they will be capital subjects for demonstrating the muscles.

Besides, the facility afforded for conveyance by steamboats is such that nothing would be more easy than to supply the whole London school from this quarter." As far as is known, no Highlander made this final journey to London. But who knows?

The West Port Murderers

The February wind blew cold as the tomb as the muffled man in the old camlet cloak trudged wearily towards Carlisle from the direction of the Scottish border. A battered hat was pulled over his dull, snake-like eyes and a thick woollen muffler hid sullen, sunken features and large, cruel mouth.

The rattling and pounding of the north-bound mail reached him and he looked up as the mud-spattered coach swept past on the road to Scotland. The driver raised his hand in salute, then froze as he recognised the brutal, foxy features of the stranger on the road. His friendly gesture turned to hate and he shook his fist. He turned to the passengers on top of the swaying coach. "Hare, it's Hare," he shouted, as the wind tore at his words. The passengers, forgetting the nagging discomfort of the long journey from London, turned and stared hard after the lonely figure.

William Hare, until ten days before, a partner in the notorious firm of Burke and Hare, the Edinburgh murderers, who, in nine short months, butchered sixteen people and sold their corpses for dissection, was walking into criminal history. The next day he was reported two miles beyond Carlisle. He obviously had not tarried long in the town, for some days earlier he had escaped the fury of a mob of 8,000 when he was recognised in a Dumfries inn. All authentic trace of Hare is lost after Carlisle, despite reports he was later thrown into a lime pit by avenging workmates, and spent the rest of his life roaming London streets a blind beggar.

Elsewhere in Scotland his wife, Margaret, and William Burke's woman, Helen McDougal, were evading lynching mobs by the skin of their decaying teeth. Both women had been responsible for wooing strangers to their death and McDougal in fact stood trial with Burke for murder, but the indictment against her was found Not Proven. "Nelly, you are out of the scrape", he told her before the judge sentenced Burke to death. McDougal was smuggled out of an Edinburgh jail in man's clothing, and was said to have died in Australia in 1868. Mrs Hare was threatened with lynching, but got off with nothing worse than being pelted with stones and snowballs when she was spotted in Glasgow on her flight to Greenock—and the first available boat to Belfast.

But one person did not vanish from public gaze. What remains of William Burke can still be seen today in the anatomical museum at Edinburgh University, alongside the Cramond murderer John Howison, the last criminal to be dissected in Scotland.

Burke, the Irish peasant from County Tyrone, whose name lives on in the English language and whose short, stocky skeleton has been kept for posterity. So, too, his plaster bust, made by the sculptor, Joseph, from a death mask taken the day after Burke was hanged. The bite of the rope shows around his thick neck. X-ray photographs of Burke's skull show conclusively that it is a genuine death mask. But there is friendly rivalry between Edinburgh University and the Royal College of Surgeons, where there is an identical bust, as to which is the original cast. He suffered the same fate as his victims; he was dissected. Afterwards his skin, tanned dark brown and tough as leather, was used to fashion wallets and tobacco pouches. There is a portrait of John Chiene, a fellow of Edinburgh's Royal College of Surgeons, holding such a wallet in his hand.

Burke and Hare hold a special place in British legal history. Hare saved his neck by turning King's Evidence. They have at least one Edinburgh public house named after them. Their ghoulish activities have thrilled cinemagoers over the years. And their wax effigies have an ever-lasting pitch in Madame Tussaud's Chamber of Horrors. The head of Burke was a death mask taken by Madame Tussaud three hours after his execution. Hare was modelled from life in Calton Jail, Edinburgh, before his release. Both waxworks are bearded, although in sketches at the time of the trial show the men to be clean shaven. It is possible Hare grew a beard in the weeks before his release, so that he might not be easily recognised.

The sinister pair were not resurrectionists in the truest sense of the word. As far as it is known they never robbed a grave, although Burke was supposed to have regularly watched funerals from the window of a house overlooking Greyfriars Kirkyard. Perhaps he wanted to substantiate a claim erroneously made by neighbours that he and his friend were body-snatchers.

The first man to die in Hare's lodging house in Tanner's Close and to be sold to Dr Knox expired peacefully. He was an old soldier called Donald, who died of drink and neglect, and owing his landlord £4. It was Hare who had the bright idea of selling the corpse to the doctors, and, needing an accomplice, explained the plan to his lodger, William Burke. After the parish undertaker had nailed down the coffin, Burke and Hare prised it open and substituted tanner's bark for the old man.

After dark on November 29, 1827 they delivered the goods, in a sack to Number 10 Surgeons' Square, which stood next door to the Royal Medical Society's premises. Knox and his assistant paid £7 10s for the thing in the sack. Burke and Hare were in business. It was to last for nine months and their dark dealings became known as 'The West Port Murders', although not all their victims were murdered in Tanner's Close. Nine were killed in Hare's seedy lodging house, two in the adjoining stables, four in Burke's room in a tenement at the rear of the Close and one in his brother's house in Gibb's Court in the

Canongate. The trick of the trade was to lure lost and wayward men and women, and in one case a 12-year-old boy, to their lair. Burke snapped the boy's spine, but the others were all plied with drink and as they lay senseless the two murderers would smother the victim. One would squeeze the victim's mouth and nose, while his partner bounced heavily on top of the doomed person.

As business flourished, they entered into a contract with Knox and his helpers; £10 for 'subjects' delivered in the winter and £8 in the summer months. Hare's wife always got £1 of Burke's share as some sort of tax for allowing her home for murder. In his confession (he made two) Burke said he refused to pay up after one murder, and Mrs Hare refused to speak to him for three weeks. Incredible as it may seem, Dr Knox later claimed he was ignorant as to how Burke and Hare came by the bodies. The medical world was not willing to completely whitewash him. The mob had no doubts that Knox was to blame. Burke told his jailers that it was 'God's providence' that put a stop to their murdering career as they were prepared to attack people in the streets to get fresh subjects for the doctor's 'table'. There was a ready market, and they claimed the anatomists asked no questions and that when they delivered a body 'they were always told to get more'.

As all the world thrilled at the ghoulish behaviour of the two Irishmen, the urchins of Edinburgh composed a macabre ditty:

> Down the close and up the stair,
> But and ben wi' Burke and Hare.
> Burke's the butcher, Hare's the thief,
> Knox's the man who buys the beef.

The West Port, the haunt of Burke and Hare, lies a little off Edinburgh's Grassmarket, the melancholy open space below the southern crags of Edinburgh Castle. This place was used as an execution spot for more than 200 years and Sir Walter Scott wrote of the terror he experienced as a schoolboy when he and his classmates passed the spot on the day a criminal was to hang. On execution days a 'huge black gallows-tree' was erected towards the end of the Grassmarket.

"This ill-omened apparition was of great height, with a scaffold surrounding it, and a double ladder placed against it, for the ascent of the unhappy criminal and the executioner. As this apparatus was always arranged before dawn it seemed as if the gallows had grown out of the earth in the course of one night, like the production of some foul demon; and I well remember the fright with which the schoolboys, when I was one of their number, used to regard these ominous signs of deadly preparation." On the night after the hanging the gallows would again disappear to be deposited in the vaults under Parliament House or the Courts of Justice.

Long before Burke and Hare loomed on the West Port scene, the district, with its narrow, winding closes and stairways, had an evil reputation. Terrifying legends of witches, phantom coaches, ghosts and devils conjured up by the sinister Major Thomas Weir, a Presbyterian who led Montrose to the scaffold, and who was burned at the stake for witchcraft. Opposite the old gallows stone Captain John Porteous, the unpopular officer of the city's guard, was hanged over a dyer's pole by a mob, inflamed when he was pardoned for murder.

It was the building of the Union Canal between Edinburgh and Glasgow which attracted Burke and Hare to Scotland at the beginning of the nineteenth century. Burke, born in the poor parish of Orrey in County Tyrone in 1792, joined the Donegal Militia at the age of 19 and served as a batman. His brother, Constantine, was in the same regiment. After leaving the army Burke married and had a number of children, but he deserted his family and landed in Scotland in 1818 to work

7

on the construction of the Union Canal. In the village of Mad-
diston he met up with Helen McDougal and, after wandering
around Central Scotland buying and selling rags, they arrived
in the Scottish capital in 1827. Fate led them to Hare's den,
the wretched, single-storeyed house in Tanner's Close, with a
faded notice, 'Beds to Let' in the dust-coated window. Hare had
'inherited' the house from a fellow Irishman. When this man
died Hare chose his widow as his common-law wife and continued to charge lodgers the tariff of 3d each to share a bug-
infested bed with other tramps. Burke and McDougal became
paying guests, but later moved to another hovel in the West
Port when the partners quarrelled.

The first victim would appear to have been a man called
Joseph, who was dying of fever, but hurried into eternity by the
murderers with the help of a pillow. The transaction made them
£10 richer.

The second to die was a nameless Englishman who at one
time sold matches in Old Edinburgh. Their first woman victim
was a pensioner, Abigail Simpson, lured to Tanner's Close with
the promise of a drink. After suffocating the old woman they
stripped her naked and packed her in a tea chest. A porter
collected the body behind the castle and they went with him to
Surgeons' Square. "Dr Knox approved of its being so fresh, but
did not ask any questions," Burke confessed to police.

Next on the list were two nameless women, then followed,
"first ae drunk auld wife, and then anither drunk auld wife, and
then a third drunk auld wife, and then a drunk auld or sick
man or twa' ". The cruellest murder committed took place about
midsummer 1828 when a woman, with a small boy—a deaf
mute—were lured to the lodging house, on the strength of
Burke knowing the whereabouts of a family she had tramped
from Glasgow to meet. While the monsters suffocated the
woman behind a bolted door, their womenfolk looked after the
youngster. Rather than risk 'losing' the boy among the back

streets of the city they decided to kill him, too. Burke cold-bloodedly broke the boy's back over his knee and later confessed that the expression in the youngster's eyes would haunt him to his dying day. That did not stop him from tossing the boy and the woman, probably his grandmother, into a herring barrel and exchanging them for £16 at Dr Knox's rooms. The poor horse which collapsed pulling the laden cart was also sold —to a knacker!

The partners split temporarily when Burke and his woman returned from a holiday in Falkirk to discover Hare had been doing a little business on the side. The Burkes moved into new lodgings, two closes to the east of Tanner's Close, to a house which could be reached from Hare's house across open waste ground. To show there were no hard feelings they soon patched up their row and began where they left off, although the Burkes stayed in their own lodgings. After their reunion they picked their next victim, Ann McDougal, a cousin of Helen McDougal's husband. The girl came from Falkirk on a visit to Edinburgh, no doubt as a result of the Burke's stay in her home town. Even after she was reduced to helplessness by drink, Burke's feelings got the better of him and he told Hare to do the deed "she being a distant friend, he did not like to begin first on her". On this occasion the murderers were almost caught. For Burke's landlord grew suspicious of the girl's sudden disappearance and they gave him £3, in advance rent. The man left town in a hurry. Maybe he thought he would be next for carving?

About this time they disposed of an old lady, Mrs Mary Haldane, and her daughter, Peggy, who had come looking for her missing mother a few days after. Poor Mrs Haldane was being teased by urchins when her former landlord spotted her plight and hurried to the 'rescue'. The landlord was Hare, who promptly escorted Mary back to the Close, fed her whisky, then smothered her as she slept it off in the straw in the stable. Soon the inquisitive Peggy traced her to Hare's house where she was given a warm welcome by the women of the household. Burke and Hare were also in the house and soon the inevitable bottle appeared. That afternoon Peggy joined what was left of her mother in Surgeons' Square.

Burke, like the woman McDougal, stood trial on three charges of murder. He was found guilty of only one, the murder of Madgy Docherty, an Irish beggarwoman he picked up in a pub on Halloween 1828, and whose bloody corpse was traced to a tea chest deep in Dr Knox's cellar, two days later. Evidence was not led regarding the two other murders, the victims of which were two of Old Edinburgh's best known characters.

'A Grand Public Exhibition'

Mary Paterson was a beautiful, shapely Edinburgh prostitute. So well known that she was recognised by a number of medical students as she lay lifeless on the dissecting table after her murder. Before Dr Knox set to work he brought along an artist to look at her, and several sketches, still in existence, were made of the once pretty girl. She was certainly full of life when she and a girl friend, Janet Brown, entered a spirit dealer's shop in the Canongate in search of booze. One of the customers in the shop that morning of April 8, 1828 was William Burke, who soon struck up a conversation with the two 18-year-old girls and bought them drinks. Burke had already noted down the girls as his next victims and told Mary a wild story about taking her back to his lodgings to be his housekeeper. He took the girls straight to his brother Constantine's spartan single-room in Gibb's Close. Mary fell dead drunk, while Burke tried to woo her companion on a rickety bed. They were surprised during their clumsy love-play by Helen McDougal and in the blazing row that followed Burke threw a tumbler at his woman. Janet Brown slipped away to her former landlady's house and blurted out her tale. Twenty minutes later she again returned to Gibb's Close, and for the second time faced the spider in his parlour.

Unknown to her, Mary Paterson's still warm body lay a few feet away on a bed covered with a sheet. Luckily, her landlady's maid called at the house at the right moment and Janet escaped the grasping clutches of the murderers. When Burke and Hare first went into partnership they conducted their business after dark. But after they had murdered the prostitute Paterson they became bolder and carried her body to the anatomical theatre four hours after her death, and in broad daylight. Burke was to recall how they were followed by children chanting, "They are carrying a corpse."

Because of her beauty, the corpse was kept in whisky for three months before she was dissected. But Dr Knox still only paid £10 for her. One of his students wrote of the girl: "Her body could not fail to attract attention by its voluptious form and beauty; students crowded around the table on which she lay, and artists came to study a model worthy of Phidias and the best Greek art." Burke was later questioned by the doctors as to the cause of Mary's death. He told them he had bought the corpse from an old woman and that Paterson had drank herself to death.

Daft Jamie, real name James Wilson, was an 18-year-old simpleton who wandered the streets of Edinburgh, amusing citizens with his riddles; running from fights with 7-year-olds, or looking for his mother. In Burke's confessions, Daft Jamie was led to Tanner's Close by Mrs Hare like "a dumb lamb to the slaughter and as a sheep to the shearers". Mrs Hare locked the door on Daft Jamie, leaving her husband and Burke to deal with him.

The lad may have turned his back on a challenge to fight from a schoolboy, but on this occasion he put up a great fight against the murderers. But the odds were too high. After they had suffocated poor Jamie they fell on his body like vultures, robbing him of snuffbox and spoon, which had been his dearest possessions. They stripped his tattered clothes from his back and gave them to Constantine Burke's naked brats.

Although Daft Jamie and his exploits were well-known to Edinburgh folk, Dr Knox and his assistants appear to have said nothing when his body was dumped on their doorstep, so to speak. But the next day when he tumbled out of the tea-box some of the students instantly recognised him, although "Dr Knox all along persisted it was not Jamie". Daft Jamie's head and deformed feet were swiftly severed. While Burke and Hare drank the £10 fee, Jamie's mother searched the streets and closes for her son. When it later became known that the harmless creature had fallen prey to the killers, there was a bloodthirsty cry from the Edinburgh mob, directed at them and the anatomists. After this murder no doubt Burke found some solace in the religious pamphlets he kept or at the gospel meetings he attended in the Grassmarket.

By the end of nine months the partners had thoughts of expansion and planned to bring another man into their scheme. Their plan was for Burke and the new partner to go to Glasgow or Ireland, find fresh corpses, and export them to Hare, who would sell them to Dr Knox. But the murderers became greedy, and careless, and they stalked their last victim, Madgy Docherty, on Friday, October 31, 1828. Halloween, the night of the demons.

As the wind howled in the chimney pots and wailed like an army of banshees through the dark, evil-smelling closes, Mrs Docherty was enjoying her last night on earth in Burke's room. Earlier that day Burke was relishing his favourite drink of rum and bitters in the liquor shop at the mouth of Tanner's Close, when the poor woman came a-begging.

To him it was another £10 which came walking in; she was the perfect victim. A lonely stranger in town in search of a long lost son. Burke opened his heart to the little old lady and took her by the hand to his house. But the Burkes had other guests, a former soldier, James Gray, and his wife and their child, who were obviously down on the 'murder list'. They agreed to move to Hare's lodgings and Docherty stayed with Burke and McDougal.

With the Grays gone, the Burkes threw a party for their new

guest's benefit. Whisky and tales of Halloween flowed, and soon everybody was dancing. Neighbours from across the narrow passage joined in the merriment but later left for bed. At around midnight the laughter in the basement turned to shouts of anger; the raised voices of Burke and Hare, the noise of a fight, then the stifled cry of 'Murder!', followed by frantic thumping on the inside of the door. One neighbour rushed into the darkened streets to fetch a policeman, but slunk off to bed without finding one. By this time all was quiet in the Burke household.

When the Grays called at the flat for breakfast they were told Docherty had been kicked out into the streets when she became too friendly with her host. But the Grays' suspicions were aroused when Mrs Gray, edging towards a heap of straw in the corner of the room, was roughly told by Burke to keep clear. Shortly after Burke began playing the fool by sprinkling whisky all over the room and rickety furniture giving the reason he wanted the bottle empty so that he would be able to get more. And even that seemed plain daft to the Grays.

In the late afternoon Burke left Helen McDougal with the Grays while he went for more drink. It was a fatal mistake. For when they were left alone the Greys poked about the straw and uncovered Docherty's naked corpse. As they rushed from the house of horror they met McDougal, who, on realising the game was up, implored them to stay. She told them that "if they would be quiet, it would be worth £10 a week to them". But the Grays refused to be tempted and reported the facts to the police. That night the constables swooped on Burke's house and after a brief search found Docherty's bloodstained clothes, but no body. Burke and his female accomplice were arrested and taken to the Tolbooth. The next day the Hares were taken into custody, hotly denying any knowledge of the crime.

About the same time the police called at Dr Knox's rooms in Surgeons' Square, where the inevitable tea chest was opened to reveal the dead Docherty. But when the Burkes and Hares were later shown the body at the police station they claimed they did not know the woman. Next morning the *Edinburgh Evening Courant* carried the first story on the Burke and Hare horrors under a far from circulation-chasing headline, 'Extraordinary Occurrence'. Readers were told of the discovery of the body in the anatomy theatre and of the arrest of certain persons. Horrifying rumours swept the city but, as it turned out, fact was to be far more gruesome than fiction.

Burke told a fantastic story to the examining sheriff as to how Mrs Docherty came to be hidden in his room. It began with a stranger lugging a tea-box into the house and asking Burke to repair some shoes. As Burke busied himself with his less-lucrative sideline of cobbling, the man unhitched the rope around the box and bent over the pile of straw. After the stranger left Burke uncovered the corpse. He strongly objected when the man obligingly returned and the body was removed. That was Burke's story and he stuck to it until he made his confessions in the condemned cell. McDougal claimed Mrs Docherty had been thrown out of the house when she became troublesome and pleaded innocence when asked how the body came to be in the room.

The Hares also made statements, but, because Burke's partner decided to turn King's Evidence, their versions were never made public. In fact, the initial inquiries by police and sheriff were kept secret from inquisitive scribes. The legal experts were in a quandary as the four prisoners despite repeated examination, refused to co-operate. The Lord Advocate therefore had no choice but to spare some of the accused and allow them to give witness against each other. Burke was up to his neck in the affair, so Hare was chosen, and also his wife, who could not in law give evidence against her husband. The first thing Hare did was to implicate his old friends in the murders of Mary Paterson and Daft Jamie.

When the trial of Burke and McDougal opened at the Justiciary Courthouse on Christmas Eve all Edinburgh seemed to be there. The court room was crowded to near suffocation by people who had queued from dawn to get inside. After a lengthy legal debate the Court ruled that the charges should be tried separately, and the Lord Advocate decided to deal with the third charge first, the murder of Mrs Docherty. The Crown case was at its strongest here.

The court sat without a break for the next twenty-four hours and did not rise until after the Justice Clerk, Lord Boyle, donned the black cap and pronounced the death sentence on Burke. Because of the stench in the packed courtroom, the windows were thrown open for the whole trial, and rain and chill winds beat down on the judges and lawyers, who looked like hooded monks as they covered their be-wigged heads with their robes for protection. The only doubt the court had was whether Burke should be exhibited in chains. But the sentence was that he should be hanged and later publicly dissected and anatomised. The Judge told Burke: "I trust that if it is ever customary to preserve skeletons, yours will be preserved, in order that posterity may keep in remembrance your atrocious crimes." The anatomists eagerly pounced on the judge's suggestion, and that is why his skeleton has found a resting place in Edinburgh's anatomical museum.

There was a great outcry from various quarters at the end of the trial, for many key witnesses were never called, including Dr Knox and three of his assistants. The newspapers bayed for Knox's blood, although they had little to complain of when it came to counting circulation; extra copies sold by the *Edinburgh Evening Courant* numbered 8,000. Feeling was high throughout Scotland that the anatomists should have been called to the witness box, and that Hare should be brought to trial. It never happened. Attempts by Daft Jamie's mother to bring a private prosecution of murder against Hare failed. So too did a civil action for £500 damages against him, solely because the Wilsons could never expect the penniless murderer to pay up.

In the death cell at Calton Jail. Burke was closely watched as he threatened to cheat the hangman by his own hand. He reflected on his past crimes, and in one instance moaned that Hare still owed him £5 for his 'share' of Mrs Docherty. Early on Tuesday, January 27, 1829, he was taken by coach to a cell in Liberton's Wynd, just a few paces from where they were erecting the gallows in the Lawnmarket. Rain clouds pressed low and black over Edinburgh the following morning, and, despite torrential rain, a huge crowd, estimated at 25,000, came from far and near. They clambered on the high, wet roofs overlooking the execution spot and some people paid between 5s and 10s for a ringside seat at the tenement windows. Burke was to meet the hangman on two occasions. He bumped into him in a corridor shortly before the execution. Burke told him, "I'm not ready for you, yet."

At eight o'clock Burke drank a glass of wine and then walked up Liberton's Wynd to his death, jeered by the mob. They roared: "Bring out Hare" and "Hang Knox!". On the scaffold Burke remained as cool, even while giving his devotions with Catholic priests.

Burke spoke only three words. As the hangman Williams adjusted the doomed man's blindfold he told him, "The knot's behind." At 8.15 a.m. he gave the signal, and died without a struggle. The crowd pressed forward to get a souvenir, and a wild scramble took place with people cutting portions of the rope, and grabbing the shavings from the coffin. Fifty minutes later Burke was cut down and during the night was removed to Professor Monro's rooms in the college. The following day the body was dissected, as a riot raged both inside and outside the building. Tickets were issued to important citizens and medical students, but hundreds more were locked out. Police were summoned as the angry students smashed the windows of the anatomical theatre, and batons were wielded with great force and accuracy. But a university professor took the situation in hand and arranged for the students to be allowed inside the theatre in batches of fifty.

Edinburgh was treated to a grisly spectacle the following day when "a grand public exhibition" was made of Burke's remains. From morning till dusk more than 30,000 people passed through the anatomical theatre to stare at the body on the black marble slab. Sir Walter Scott wrote of the macabre spectacle: "The corpse of the murderer Burke is now lying in state at the College, in the anatomical class, and all the world flock to see him. Who is he that says we are not ill to please in our objects of curiosity? The strange means by which the wretch made money are scarce more disgusting that the eager curiosity with which the public have licked up all the carrion details of this business." The next day thousands more queued outside the college, but the university authorities decided not to repeat the 'side-show', and afterwards further dissected and pickled the body.

On 5 February, 1829 Hare was released from Calton Jail and was put on the southward mail. As far as his fellow passengers knew, his name was 'Mr Black', but when the travellers took a short break at an inn he was recognised by a lawyer who had acted for Daft Jamie's folk. When the coach pulled in at Dumfries, news of the infamous passenger swept through the town and an 8,000 strong crowd blocked the street outside the King's Arms, where Hare and his wary fellow passengers warmed themselves in front of the fire.

At first the mob that spilled into the inn appeared to be friendly and he accepted their drink, but refused to answer their questions. But their mood quickly changed, and the local police arrived in time to save him from lynching. The magistrates called a hurried meeting and played two ruses on the seething crowd; first sending an empty coach off towards the south, and then a small gig, also empty. These diversions gave Hare the chance to jump from a back window and make a run for the Dumfries jailhouse. He slept peacefully behind bars that night as the crowd howled for his blood and wrecked lamplights and windows. He was sent on his way before the grey light of dawn, and, as we have seen, he was last spotted beyond Carlisle. It is possible that Hare returned to his native land, for during the weeks before his release from Calton Jail he told fellow prisoners that he meant to head for Ireland when free.

From their dark deeds there came some good. It goaded the Government into passing the Anatomy Act. Today there is no trace of Tanner's Close. Hare's squalid lodging house was swept away in 1902, but the stables remained long after to become one of Edinburgh's first garages. In recent years the demolition squads moved in to make room for Argyle House, a multi-storeyed Government building, which rises like a white tombstone over the old town. But Burke's memorial is his own skeleton, suspended in its show case at the anatomical museum. And, in a way, the museum itself.

The Anatomist

"Hang Burke, banish Hare,
Burn Knox in Surgeons' Square."—*Children's rhyme*

Had not Burke and Hare, looking for a market for their first subject, met one of Dr Knox's students in Old College Square on the South Bridge, they would have probably taken their custom elsewhere. They asked directions to Professor Alexander Monro's rooms, but he told them to go to Dr Knox. Not that Professor Monro, or any other anatomist, would have turned them away. The murderers, known later as 'John' and 'William' to the students, met Knox's three principal assistants, Thomas Jones, William Fergusson and Alexander Miller, and later returned with the body of Donald the old soldier who faded away, and clinched the deal.

When the scandal broke like a thunderstorm upon Edinburgh, Knox earnestly believed that "the matter would subside in a short while". He was a brave man, but he was also egotistic and vain, and paid no apparent attention to the mood of the citizens. A statement that Knox had conducted himself with the 'utmost civility' towards constables who went to Surgeons' Square in search of the last victim was disputed by the Edinburgh press. The *Caledonian Mercury* claimed that the fact was that he "swore at them from his window, and threatened to blow their brains out; and it was only upon their proceedings to force the door of his lecture room, that it was opened by one of the keepers".

His surgical brethren had little love for this man who arrogantly claimed kinship with John Knox. They hated him for his manner and his flashy dress. Knox, who was born in Edinburgh, had served six years as an army surgeon with the 72nd Highlanders, mostly in the Cape Peninsula.

He also attended the Waterloo wounded. He had picked up a swagger from his army years, and his taste in dress was more ostentatious than anything his fellow anatomists would dream of wearing. He had a liking for bright waistcoats, embroidered with purple, and sparkled with gold watch chains and diamonds.

Knox was always a highly controversial figure on the Edinburgh medical scene. During his lectures he sneered and jibed at rival teachers, and he once referred to an operation conducted by Liston as a combination of "brute force, ignorance and presumption".

Yet he was a brilliant anatomist, who demanded his faithful students should receive only the best. He paid nearly £800 from his own pocket to keep up the supply of bodies and his reward was attendances of between 300 and 400 pupils, three-quarters of the medical school roll. In 1828 the figure reached 500; the largest anatomical class ever to gather in Britain.

The surgeon had begun his winter lectures on surgery and practical anatomy and operative surgery during the winter the Burke and Hare scandal broke, and attendances were the highest ever. In return for an additional fee of three guineas per student, he advertised that "arrangements have been made to secure as usual an ample supply of anatomical subjects". At his first lecture following the trial he told his students: "I will do just a I have done heretofore." The people who attended his classes were not only medical students; many were clergymen, barristers, scholars, noblemen and artists.

But the newspapers were hounding him continuously. The *Caledonian Mercury*, in demanding an investigation into the running of medical schools, commented: "The public can have no authentic and satisfactory knowledge of this without a full and complete investigation; they can have no guarantee that every anatomical teacher in Edinburgh has not a Burke in his pay at the moment. The present impression on the minds of the people is, that one gentleman stands in the same relation to Burke that the murderers of Banquo did to Macbeth."

The *Edinburgh Weekly Chronicle* was even more blunt: "In purchasing the bodies which had come under the fell gripe of the Burkes and the Hares, there must have been an utter reck-lessness, a thorough indifference as to the causes and conse-quences, which, in point of criminality, very closely borders upon guilty knowledges."

But Knox's brother surgeons were adopting a holier-than-he attitude, and refused to defend him.

On Thursday, February 12, the press leaked information that Knox had asked ten gentlemen, headed by the Marquis of Queensferry, to make an impartial, but private, inquiry into his conduct. This was the signal for day-long demonstrations by the Edinburgh mob, beginning with a march headed by a gang of ruffians carrying an effigy labelled, "Knox, the associate of the infamous Hare". Outside Knox's house at 4 Newington Place they hung the dummy on a tree then set it alight. The mob stoned the house, shattering windows, then injured a policeman who tried to intervene.

Knox, cool as ever, slipped out of the back door to go to dinner in St Patrick's Square, armed with a sword, pistols and a dirk. While he was dining with a doctor friend, a second mob had swooped on Newington Place and smashed the remaining window panes in the doctor's home. The rioting lasted one night only, but in the following weeks Knox had to be escorted to and from Surgeons' Square by his students in case he should be ambushed.

In the middle of March 1829 the *Caledonian Mercury* published a letter from Dr Knox, and the result of the inquiry by the committee, from which the Marquis of Queensferry had resigned.

The committee cleared Knox and his assistants of any knowledge of the Burke and Hare murders, but they thought the doctor "had acted in a very incautious manner" in receiving the bodies and they regarded as 'unfortunate' his direction to his assistants to make no inquiries of persons bringing bodies, as likely to "diminish or divert the supply of subjects".

It found that "by the laxity of the regulations under which bodies were received into his rooms, he unintentionally gave a degree of facility to the disposal of the victims of their crimes, which under better regulations would not have existed, and which is doubtless matter of deep and lasting regret, not only to himself but to all who have reflected on the importance and are therefore interested in the prosecution of the study of anatomy".

In his own letter, Knox observed: "I cannot be supposed to be a candid judge of my own case, and therefore it is extremely probable that any opinion of mine on the last view adopted by the committee is incorrect and theirs right. If it be so, I most willingly submit to the censure they have inflicted, and shall hold it my duty to profit from it by due care hereafter. My consolation is, that I have at least not been obstinate in my errors, and that no sanction has ever been given in any fair quarter to the most serious imputations by which it has been the interest of certain persons to assail me. Candid men will judge of me according to the wisdom which has unexpectedly been acquired since. This is the very first time that I have ever made any statement to the public in my own vindication, and it shall be the last."

David Paterson, doorkeeper and general handyman at 10 Surgeons' Square, also turned against his master. In a letter to the *Caledonian Mercury* he protested his innocence of the whole affair and threw the blame on Dr Knox. But the newspaper promptly accused him of having within an hour of Mrs Docherty's death offered her body for sale to "a highly respectable lecturer on anatomy" for £15 because Dr Knox would give Burke and Hare only £12.

Paterson, in reply, admitted an attempted deal, but denied that the corpse was that of Mrs Docherty. He claimed the body was one the professional resurrectionist, Merry Andrew, had promised to supply. In the weeks to come, Paterson tried to sell Sir Walter Scott a selection of anecdotes on body-snatching, but the outraged author denounced Paterson as "Dr Knox's jackal for buying murdered bodies". Loyal assistants of Knox later claimed that Paterson had intended entering into business with either Burke or Hare to go to Ireland to procure bodies.

In the years that followed, Knox's classes began to lose numbers, alarmingly. He was a shunned man, but he refused to be forced into an early retirement. In 1831 he kept himself and his few remaining students busy probing a gigantic whale cast up at North Berwick. The monster was 78ft long and weighed 28 tons, but they managed to transport it to the Royal Scottish Museum in Edinburgh. But Knox was far less successful in other fields. In 1835, with class numbers dropping daily, he applied for the Chair of Pathology and Chair of Physiology at Edinburgh, but was unsuccessful, because he was thought to be radical and lacking in essential 'Calvinistic credentials'.

The bitter truth was that no Scottish university would have him. Although he was a leading authority on his subject, he found no favour even as a lecturer in anatomy to Edinburgh's art students. Among his accusers was Sir Walter Scott and Professor Wilson (Christopher North) who urged in *Blackwood's Magazine*: "He is ordered to open his mouth and speak, or be for ever dumb." In desperation, Knox moved to Glasgow in 1844; but his classes there were so small that he gave his students their fees back. Shunned by his fellow Scots, he went on to London, where he kept himself from starving by lecturing and journalism and by writing books which later became best sellers and standard reference works.

But he had his supporters. Lord Cockburn wrote of the affair: "All our anatomists incurred a most injust, and a very alarming though not unnatural odium; Dr Knox in particular against whom not only the anger of the populace, but the condemnation of more intelligent persons, was specially directed. But tried in reference to the invariable, and the necessary practice of the profession, our anatomists were spotlessly correct, and Knox most correct of them all."

Knox was later struck off the roll of the Royal Society of Edinburgh for being in arrears with his subscription, and later dismissed by the Royal College of Surgeons. In the twilight of his life Knox operated a small practice in Hackney. He was seventy-one when he died in 1862, and was buried in Woking.

Poor Knox could not escape the limelight even after death. When the Charles Denville Company performed their blood-and-thunder drama, *The Horrible Crimes of Burke and Hare* to packed houses in Glasgow's Metropole Theatre, medical students hissed and booed every time the actor who played the anatomist walked on to the stage. But perhaps they felt entitled —they had already loaned a quantity of skulls and bones as props.

Knox loved little children, but even in the end they taunted him through the streets of Edinburgh by chanting slanderous doggerel. To escape the venomous attacks heaped on him by press and public he went walking in the country with a friend. They came upon a little girl singing happily as she plucked wild flowers by the roadside. Knox stopped and spoke to the child. He said he would give her sixpence if she sang her song for him. She sang sweetly, and the anatomist promised her lots of sixpences if she came back to live with him in Edinburgh.

"Oh, no. I'd be afraid to live in Edinburgh." When the old man asked why, the girl replied, "You might sell me to Dr Knox." Knox walked slowly back to Surgeons' Square, tears brimming in his eyes.

'I'm A Bloody Body-Snatcher'

—

Autumn 1831, and the city of London had a much more gruesome attraction to offer sightseers than the Bloody Tower. They
were flocking in their hundreds to a grubby backwater in Shoreditch called Nova Scotia Gardens, where they paid to pass
through two gloomy houses and peer down a garden well. Days
before, the metropolis had been shocked and revolted to learn
that 'Burking' had come to town.

The two men responsible were London resurrectionists, John
Bishop and his brother-in-law Thomas Williams, who, in a few
short weeks, committed three murders and hawked the bodies
around medical schools. Their method was horrific, but simple;
they lured a woman and two small boys to their hovels, then
drugged and drowned them in the well. But the end came
suddenly when they tried to sell the body of their last victim,
a 14-year-old Italian boy, Carlo Ferrari, to a suspicious dissecting
room porter at King's College.

Ferrari, who earned a living of sorts by exhibiting white mice
in the streets and pubs, met the two killers in the Bell Tavern
in Smithfield late in the evening of Thursday, November 3.
They struck up a conversation with the boy and Williams promised he would find work for him. All three then left for Nova
Scotia Gardens, but on the way they made a stop at a public
house in Shoreditch where they drank stout.

When they arrived home, Bishop's wife and children and
Williams' bride of a few weeks, were still up; so they put the
boy in the privy while Williams went inside and told them to go

to bed. About fifteen minutes later, when the coast was clear, the boy was taken into the house. Lighting a candle, they gave the Italian a crust of bread and cheese. After he had eaten, they plied him with a cup filled with rum and laudanum. He drank the contents of the cup in two gulps, and afterwards had a little beer. Soon he was fast asleep on a chair and Bishop picked him up and laid him on the floor.

Bishop and Williams decided to take a stroll along to the Feathers, near Shoreditch Church, and drank a pint of beer and a quantern of gin apiece.

Bolstered by booze, they came back to the room about twenty minutes later to find the boy still snoring. They carried him insensible into the garden and tied a cord round his ankles. Bishop then took him in his arms and let him slide headlong into the dark well, while his companion fastened the other end of the rope round a pailing to prevent the boy from getting beyond their reach.

Bishop, in the confession he wrote on the eve of his execution, described in horrific detail what followed: "The boy struggled a little with his arms and legs in the water, and the water bubbled for a minute. We waited till these symptoms were past, and then went indoors, and afterwards I think we went out, and walked down Shoreditch to occupy the time, and in about three-quarters of an hour we returned and took him out of the well, by pulling him by the cord attached to his feet; we undressed him in the paved yard, rolled his clothes up, and buried them where they were found by the witness who produced them.

"We carried the boy into the washhouse, laid him on the floor, and covered him over with a bag. We left him there, and went and had some coffee in Old Street Road, and then (a little before two o'clock on the morning of Friday) went back to my house. We immediately doubled the body up, and put it into a box, which we corded, so that nobody might open it to see what was in it, and then we went again, and had some more coffee at the same place in Old Street Road, where we stayed a little while, and then went home to bed. . . ."

At eleven o'clock on the Friday morning the cold-blooded killers went for more drink, but this time they chose the Fortune of War public house. a favourite haunt of the London resurrectionists. The pub was next door to Smithfield meat market, where brawny porters could be hired to carry heavy loads and ask no questions. And there was a room inside the pub where hampers could be left while the body-snatchers went across the road to do business at St Bartholomew's Hospital.

After sharing a pot or two of ale with cronies, and talking about the current market price for 'subjects', they went canvassing in the West End. They went first to Windmill Street, where they tried to sell the body to Mr Tuson, at the anatomical school there. But Tuson refreshed their memories about their unreliability; they had failed to deliver a body they had promised the week before.

Next stop was J. C. Carpue's anatomical school in Dean Street. After assuring the lecturer the body was fresh, Carpue knocked the asking price down from ten to eight guineas. Business done, they returned to the Fortune of War, where they bought drinks for John May, who had started life as a solicitor's clerk, but was sacked for drunkenness, so turned to body-snatching.

Bishop wondered if perhaps they had let the body at too cheap a price, so they consulted May. He told him he had sold two subjects at Guy's Hospital that morning for ten guineas each. Bishop told him about Carpue's offer, but May insisted he would get more for the body of a young boy. Bishop then invited May to handle the deal and told him he could keep anything over nine guineas.

They then took a cab back to Nova Scotia Gardens, and, after wrenching the teeth from the Italian boy's head, they took the body in a sack to Guy's. But there was no sale there, or at

Grainger's anatomical theatre, so that night was spent in drinking at the Fortune of War.

At eight o'clock the next morning they were again sinking pints in the Fortune of War; but they later visited the anatomical department of King's College. After haggling over the price, it was agreed to part with the body for nine guineas. They returned in the afternoon with the tell-tale hamper and rolled the tiny corpse at the feet of the porter. He was immediately on his guard. It was obvious to him that the body had never been buried; the limbs were rigid, the left arm bent, one hand was tightly clenched and there was blood on the forehead.

The porter hurried off to fetch Mr Partridge, the lecturer, who delayed the resurrectionists long enough for the police to arrive. The men were drunk and furious and the constables had a struggle in arresting them. May was fighting drunk and had to be dragged into the police station with his smock frock pulled over his head to stop him biting. In the charge room, Bishop, when asked his trade, screamed: "I'm a bloody body-snatcher!"

Police searched the house in Nova Scotia Gardens, and found not only the tools used by resurrectionists, but a brown hairy cap and a pair of bloodstained breeches that had belonged to the Italian boy. Bishop's children were toying with his white mice. Digging in the garden they found more clothing, and in the privy of the derelict house next door they discovered a bundle of woman's clothes.

Bishop, Williams and May were tried at the Old Bailey on Friday, December 2, 1831; a distinguished spectator was His Royal Highness the Duke of Sussex. They were charged with the murder of Carlo Ferrari, and another boy, but not with the woman, Frances Pigburn. They were found guilty. May wailed: "I am a murdered man." Snarled Williams: "We are all murdered men."

On the eve of the execution, Bishop also confessed to the murder of Frances Pigburn, who they picked up wandering the streets of Shoreditch and had taken back to the old house adjoining their home. In the darkness, they gave the woman a bottle of rum mixed with laudanum to drink. "She sat down on the steps between the two rooms in the house, and went off to sleep in about ten minutes. She was falling back; I caught her, to save her fall, and she lay with her back on the floor. Then Williams and I went to a public house, got something to drink, and in about half an hour came back to the woman. We took her cloak off, tied a cord to her feet, carried her to the well in the garden, and thrust her into it headlong. She struggled very little afterwards, and the water bubbled a little at the top. . . ."

The dramatic confessions meant a reprieve for May, but on hearing the news he collapsed in a fit on the floor of his cell and died a few months later.

On Monday, December 5, Bishop and Williams were hanged at Newgate Jail amid scenes of tremendous excitement. More than two hundred police were on duty as the crowd, estimated at 100,000 by contemporary newspapers, choked the streets leading to the scaffold.

In Giltspur Street a barrier collapsed under the pressure and a large number of spectators and police were crushed. At eight o'clock the hangman and his assistants stepped on to the scaffold, followed by the two body-snatchers. The signal was given, and they died. The bodies were left hanging for an hour before being cut down and carted off to the anatomists. William's body was sent to St Bart's, and Bishop's, with a touch of irony, was sent to King's College for dissection.

'Clever, Dirty Andrew Moir'

The *Aberdeen Lancet* informed its readers in June 1831 of a 'demoralising system' among medical students at the university: that for many years poorer students had "frequently procured bodies, not only for the lecturers, but for the purpose of sale to their more fortunate brethren".

Andrew Moir was almost certainly one of the resurrectionists who foraged for bodies to help swell his meagre income and his knowledge of the human body. He soon outstripped the knowledge of his teachers and later became a brilliant anatomist, despite opposition from jealous rivals. The *Lancet,* the highly-controversial mouthpiece of the Aberdeen medical world, said of him: "Although he was unrecognised at first by any college or corporation in the kingdom, he drew over to himself the majority of the medical students of this place, and by his zeal, industry and perseverance, raised up to himself in a short time a character as a teacher of anatomy which it is but small justice to him to say has never been equalled in this town."

But Dr Moir never looked for fame and fortune in his field, and remained as poor as some of his students. It had been so since he was born in Aberdeen in 1806. His family was poor, and in later years his father was sexton at Nellfield Cemetery. Three at least of the Moir family became university graduates: one in divinity and two in medicine. Andrew himself was intended for the church, and for a time he mingled his two studies of anatomy and divinity, studying anatomy at Marischal College and divinity at Kings. After a dissection he used to be seen hastily wiping his hands saying: "I must be off to read my Exegesis in the Old Town." But after two years he concentrated on medicine after securing a medical apprentice fee.

The young genius and his colleagues had to struggle with the heavy burden of incompetent and indifferent lecturers, a hostile public and rivalry of inter-university factions. Where the basic medical subjects were taught inefficiently the students had to rely on extra-mural lecturers, who compensated for the twice-weekly anatomical classes held at the university. One, Dr Patrick Blaikie, an ex-naval surgeon in the Napoleonic Wars, was well-known in Aberdeen for his "smuggled anatomical instruction" while still carrying out his surgical lectures. These pirate lectures took place in a house in Littlejohn Street.

Dr Moir himself said later of that period: "There was in my time no teacher who concerned himself in the least about the progress of his students, or who took any pains to instruct them. We mostly studied anatomy and practical surgery, and these we learned at the dissecting room, all groping our way as well as we could, and the older students assisting the less experienced." He described teachings in some classes as a 'mere sham'. One lecturer gave only three lectures in one year.

But Moir prevailed and, after taking the diploma of the Royal College of Surgeons of England in 1828, he applied to join the army. But there was no vacancy and he returned to Aberdeen. But first he made a fleeting visit to Paris where he did the rounds of the famous hospitals and listened to lectures by Lisfranc, Dupuytren, Larrey and other world-renowned figures. He was fascinated by The Morgue, a vacated butcher shop on the Marche-Neuf, and visited the place to inspect the bodies washed up on the Seine or found in the Paris streets. Bodies were plentiful through the indifference to human life during the Revolution and absence of inquiries into public deaths. A 'subject' could be got for less money than a porter claimed for taking a body to a medical school in Scotland. The dissecting tables at La Pitie Hospital groaned under the weight of eleven bodies a day, and with corpses costing five francs for an unopened body (three-and-a-half francs for opened bodies), life was sweet for the French medical students.

Back in Aberdeen, Dr Moir decided to become an extra-mural lecturer on anatomy and physiology, a decision that was to change his life. He had left the university in 1828 with the blessing of Professor Charles Skene, of the Chair of Medicine, and Dr Alexander Ewing, lecturer on anatomy. They gave Moir glowing testimonials and recommended him most strongly to the Director-General of the Army Medical Board. But when Andrew Moir announced his plans on his homecoming and later set up his private class, he was instantly branded by Professor Skene and Dr Ewing as a worthless character and as a common body-snatcher! He was accused of ingratitude and students were warned to keep away from his dissecting rooms in the city's Guestrow.

In disgust, Dr Moir left the city after a year and went into general practice at Kincardine o' Neil in West Aberdeenshire. But his retirement did not last long, for Moir had friends in Aberdeen and several practitioners and students urgently pleaded with him to return.

They were fed up with the lack of teaching at Marischal College and King's College, and angry at the methods employed to get Moir out of town. He relented, and was back teaching privately in Aberdeen in 1829, although both colleges refused to recognise him. But a year later his classes were given the blessing of the Royal College of Surgeons in Edinburgh and London; this meant students were able to attend his classes instead of going to the university for the diplomas.

Dr Moir would have probably made his fortune if he had remained in private practice; but as the years slipped by he became saddled with the reputation of being a resurrectionist and his few private patients refused to attend him. A sober, dedicated man he had little time for dress, even if he could have afforded the latest fashions. He was forced to do all his own teaching and demonstrating as well as clearing up the dissecting rooms, and taking part in body-snatching expeditions. His students loved him dearly. His enemies sneered at his efforts and nick-named him, 'clever, dirty Andrew Moir' because of his body-snatching activities.

He was an enthusiastic resurrectionist and insisted members of his anatomical class took their turn in digging up bodies. His assistant, Dr Paterson, moved that "every person absenting himself from depositing or taking up a dead body should be fined 10s 6d unless indisposed". Students who failed to take their turn without a reasonable excuse faced expulsion from his class. But fines were usually imposed and the money divided up among the students. On one outing Moir somehow stuck his hand in the coffin lid while he was still in the opened grave. "Heave down the earth, my lads", he called gleefully to the students. It was said he led a raiding party on his minister brother's kirkyard!

Aberdeen's medical school abounded with amateur resurrectionists, but there were only a handful of professional body-snatchers. A distinctive character was George Pirie, the sacrist at the Marischal College, who signed as witness the trust deed with the Aberdeen Medical Society in 1817, and who is frequently mentioned in the secretary's minutes as assisting in lifting of 'things', for which he got a regular fee, and in return took the students under his fatherly protection. Pirie, a jolly little man, made extra pocket money on examinations day at Marischal College by providing bursars with a welcome 'bawbee bun' and glass of water.

Two body-snatchers who worked together for many years in Aberdeenshire were Peter Brownie, a young farmer from Fintray, and the gravedigger at Newhills, known as 'Resurrectionist

Marr'. Brownie was never caught, but eventually repented to become a staunch member of the Quaker community at Kinmuck, a rural hamlet 12 miles north-west of Aberdeen. He also designed the mort-safe now in the anatomy department at Aberdeen University. Brownie died in 1886 and is buried in the Quaker kirkyard at Kinmuck.

Dr Andrew Moir's knowledge of anatomy was unsurpassed anywhere else in Britain; he revelled in the production of delicate dissections. He once told his students: "Anatomy can only be learned by dissection, and I earnestly entreat you to let slip no opportunity of improving your knowledge in this respect. Dissect even the same parts again and again until you have made yourselves complete masters of the subject." His manual dexterity was remarkable but his classroom manner was unspectacular. But many of his students gained high honours in the medical world and the great Sir Astley Cooper himself complimented the Aberdeen anatomist.

Moir was a humble, sensitive and modest man. At one of his lectures he said: "I have reason to thank my God that my wants are few and easily supplied, and that if He has made poverty my lot He has likewise given me strength to support it with a patient and equal mind."

He needed all his strength to face up to the ordeals which lurked around the corner. The first warning came at the beginning of 1829 when a watchman stumbled on a gruesome find in Aberdeen's Guestrow; a sack containing a limbless body of a man who had earlier been buried at New Deer, Aberdeenshire. At Inverurie, watchmen had set an ambush for medical students after a number of raids on the local kirkyard. Locals kept watch from The Bass, a 50 foot high mound which marks the spot of an ancient motte and bailey castle, and two students walked into the trap. But, foolishly, the townsfolk swooped before the students began digging for the corpse, and, although manhandled, the frightened students were freed the next day by the magistrates. A 'spy' was uncovered by the inhabitants and he was forced to quit the district.

Body-snatching raids intensified throughout the North-east. After a grave was rifled under the manse windows it drew a dry comment from the minister: "Nae doot it was naething but an Episcopal craiter, but, sir, it was a human bein' efter a'."

But the time for joking was over. The *Aberdeen Journal* commented after the grisly find in the Guestrow: "We had occasion before to caution resurrectionists not to tamper with the present and provoked state of public feeling; for some dreadful and summary mode of punishment will unquestionably overtake those who engage in such wanton and outrageous acts."

In March 1829, a month after Burke was hanged, Moir was singled out by the mob, when word spread that a stolen body was being dissected in his rooms. Stones had been hurled at his rooms in the past during lectures, but on this occasion the mob went much further. They swept into the building in the Guestrow and started to tear it apart; surgical instruments were destroyed, overalls ripped and window shutters and furniture smashed. A man tried to wrench the slates off the roof while others had started a bonfire in the street. The town sergeants and police arrived to break up the rioters and one man was marched off to jail. During the search of the dissecting rooms a body was found and this was taken to the Drum's Aisle in St Nicholas Church, which was used as a watch-house. While the 'subject' was being carted off to the 'Mither Kirk', some of the citizens claimed a box containing skulls had been found in the dissecting rooms.

By 1831, with the increasing success of his classes, Moir decided to get larger and more suitable premises. Several influential friends subscribed money for the erection of a special anatomical theatre. The site chosen was Hospital Row, a rough track which bi-sected a large bleaching green near the west end

of St Andrew Street, and in November 1831, Moir was deliver-
ing his first lecture in the brand-new building.

But in the following weeks a campaign of hate was mounted
against the anatomists and medical students of the city when a
wild rumour was circulated that an attempt had been made to
'Burk' two small boys in John Street, in the vicinity of the
anatomical theatre.

The damage was done in a few paragraphs in the *Aberdeen
Journal*, headed 'Supposed Attempt at Burking', in which it was
claimed the boys had been approached near the Baptist Church
by "two well dressed and rather young men" who asked the
youngsters to run an errand for which they would be well paid.

The boys followed the two men into John Street but because
the strangers were whispering together the boys took fright and
bolted. "This is the boys' simple statement, and the readers
may make any comment on it they choose", ended the short
report.

But the newspaper carried a much bigger item on the same
page; the terrible confessions of the London burkers Bishop and
Williams, and an account of their execution. The combination
of their confessions, which detailed graphically the last, horrifying moments of their victims, and the report of the alleged kid-
napping of the Aberdeen boys, was to touch off the fuse which
was to bring violent repercussions on Dr Moir and his anatomical theatre. The explosion came on Monday, December 19,
1831.

Dalmaik Kirk, Aberdeenshire. The last resting place of
'Shotty' Ross

PLATE 13

The dissection hall

PLATE 14

THE DUNECHT MYSTERY
Dunecht House, Aberdeenshire, with the Chapel in the foreground

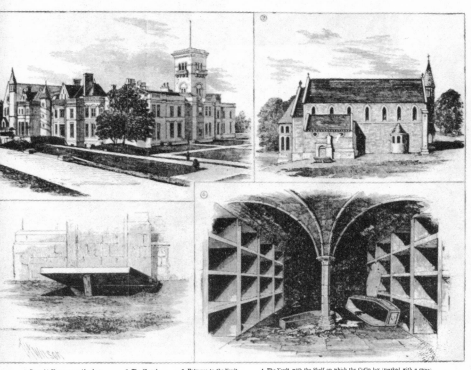

1. Dunecht House, near Aberdeen.   2. The Chapel.   3. Entrance to the Vault.   4. The Vault, with the Shelf on which the Coffin lay (marked with a cross).

The crime as depicted by *The Illustrated London News* of the time

PLATE 15

St. Nicholas Church, Aberdeen, in 1860
The 'subjects' of anatomist Dr. Andrew Moir were taken
here by the mob during the 'Burkin' Hoose' riot of 1831

St. Fittick's Kirk, Aberdeen
A favourite hunting ground of corpse-seeking medical
students of the 19th century

PLATE 16

𝔅urn, 𝔅oose, 𝔅urn

It began with a dog; an inquisitive mongrel sniffing and scraping at something in the ground at the rear of Dr Moir's anatomical theatre. The animal tugged and strained at the object and its excited barking caught the attention of a group of small urchins playing nearby. A huddle of mothers stopped their gossiping and shouted a warning to the children. The anatomical theatre, although only built a few weeks before, already had a sinister reputation. It was a forbidding building, with three 'false, church-looking windows', to discourage the over inquisitive, facing St Andrew Street. The only daylight came from windows in the back of the building and a cupola on the roof. Folk living nearby had complained of the smell from the place, which they had nicknamed the 'Burkin Hoose'.

Young men from the neighbouring tannery elbowed the children aside, and peered at what the dog was trying to unearth. By now the knot of urchins and workmen had grown to a group of about thirty, and word spread that the ground was sown with dismembered corpses. Cries of horror and anger roared out and the ringleaders began pushing past the mason's timber, stacked around the back door of the newly completed building, and forced their way inside.

Dr Moir, unaware of the trouble that brewed at his back door, was preparing for an afternoon lecture when his classroom was invaded. He and his faithful students were beaten and kicked as they withdrew reluctantly to a smaller room and locked the door. As the fury of the mob intensified, Moir and his students made their escape through an unguarded side door. The anatomist was instantly recognised and pursued along Crooked Lane, down Schoolhill and up to the Guestrow, where he reached his house at Number 63, breathless but unharmed.

Back at the 'Burkin' Hoose' the witch-hunt took a grisly turn. The rioters had burst into a dissecting room and found three corpses stretched out on wooden boards. The bodies were in various states of dissection; one had half its skull removed. By now the streets and bleachfield around the anatomical theatre were seething with a vast throng, bent on destruction. Its mood became uglier when the bodies were carried on makeshift stretchers to the Drum's Aisle.

No attempt was made to cover the mangled corpses, and the medical students' work was there for all Aberdeen to see. The macabre procession along Crooked Lane to St Nicholas Kirk heightened the mob's fury, and, for the moment, it was directed at the anatomical theatre. "Burn the hoose, down with the Burkin' Shop", screamed the mob, and attempts were made to fire the building.

In the Guestrow a crowd was baying for Dr Moir's blood and refused to budge from his front doorstep. Stones were hurled and a number of window panes smashed. The surgeon knew he had to draw the mob away from his house, and slipped from a back window to disappear into the gloomy December afternoon.

Suddenly the sky to the west glowed an angry red. Using the mason's timber, shavings, fir and tar barrel staves for fuel, the enterprising Aberdonians had set the anatomical theatre ablaze. As smoke and flames shot into the darkening sky, the mob went berserk, grabbing planks to use as levers to undermine and topple the walls.

Lord Provost James Hadden arrived at the scene with his magistrates, town sergeants and a posse of special policemen,

called the Day Patrole, and made a speech assuring the townsfolk that every inquiry would be made, and every satisfaction
afforded, if any crime had been committed by Dr Moir. He
warned them of the serious penalties they faced and made a
half-hearted attempt to read the Riot Act, the last time this
was done in Aberdeen, but his words were drowned by loud
cheers. Great tongues of fire licked the gloom; Dr Moir's beloved
building was now an inferno. The magistrates sensed the rioters
might extend their fire-raising activities to other houses in the
area, even the Medical Society's Hall itself, and word was
flashed to the troops at Castlehill Barracks.

Between ten and twenty thousand people, almost half the
population of the city, jammed the streets; cheering, chanting
and shouting their heads off.

Two hours after the dog began digging, Aberdeen's fire
brigade arrived—to find no water could be obtained. Anyway,
the rioters informed the firemen they would not be allowed to
put the fire out for anything.

As the town sergeants and constables helplessly watched the
tumult, soldiers of the 79th Regiment (Cameron Highlanders)
marched to within a few yards of the mob, but they played no
part in quelling the riot. They were halted on the other side of
the wall from St Andrew Street; in the gardens of Gordon's
Hospital, while another detachment was posted at the bottom
of Schoolhill. There was good reason for their inactivity; the last
time the army had been called out to deal with rioters in Aberdeen, there was bloodshed. The Ross and Cromarty Rangers
killed four and wounded twelve others when a hostile mob
gathered in the town's Castlegate on George III's birthday on
June 4, 1802.

The 'Burkin' Hoose' rioters soon destroyed the back wall of
the building; next they undermined the front wall, with a little
more difficulty. When they had finished the sight was awe-
inspiring, as the roof and gables formed an arch over a blazing

inferno, until the roof collapsed with a tremendous roar amidst a firework display of sparks. At eight o'clock Andrew Moir's dream was reduced to a pile of smouldering ruins.

But he and his students had other matters on their minds for, after the destruction of the anatomical theatre, the mob turned their spite on anyone remotely resembling a medical student. For the next two hours they hounded and harrassed them; a diversion had been created earlier when a student, more curious than discreet, was recognised among the crowd which encircled the blazing 'Burkin' Hoose'. "Here's ane o' the Burkin' rascals, lat's do for him next!", yelled the crowd, and he took to his heels. "Aifter him, aifter him," they screamed, as the frightened young man tore along Blackfriars Street and Schoolhill. A group of youths joined in the chase, shouting: "A Burker, a Burker, doon with the bloody rascal." He rushed into a house in Lower Schoolhill, barred the door, then jumped a few feet from a rear window into St Nicholas Churchyard, and vanished.

After escaping from what could have become his own funeral pyre, Dr Moir was later said to have spent most of the night hidden under one of the table-topped tombstones in the kirkyard. Whether he did in fact conceal himself in this way, is not certain, but a number of students were glad of tombstone hiding places during the pursuit.

But James Polson did not get off so lightly. He was set upon by an angry crowd during the night and only timely intervention by the constabulary saved him from severe injury. Dr Moir's house was still a target for abuse and extremists threatened to destroy it, but tempers cooled in the cold night air. By ten o'clock all was quiet. The following morning the crowds returned to the still smouldering ruins of the anatomical building and a bonfire was made with what was left. Some people dug for 'things' in the ground in the hope of gaining restitution at a later date.

The 'Burnin' of the Burkin' Hoose' was to become a controversial topic in North-east Scotland for many years afterwards,
but particularly among the editors of the day. At the conclusion
of their eye witness account of the destruction of Dr Moir's
anatomical theatre the *Aberdeen Journal* commented: "At any
time such a discovery as was made in this case would have
excited the public feeling, but it did so in an especial manner
on this occasion, so great a glare of attention having lately been
directed to the means by which subjects in many cases (tho' we
are convinced not in this) have been furnished to the anatomical
schools."

Andrew Moir accused the *Aberdeen Journal* of 'befriending
incendiarists', but the weekly newspaper, which had dealt
harshly with the Resurrectionists in the past, replied that the
burning of the hoose might serve as a 'warning' to the surgeon.

But the monthly *Aberdeen Magazine* sided with the doctors
and came out strongly against the mob, the Lord Provost and
his magistrates in its edition of January 1832. Which was not
too surprising as the author was a former Aberdeen University
student, who had a number of friends in medical circles.

He observed drily: "The mob, discovered that any further
continuation of Mr Moir's course of anatomical lectures and
demonstration must be highly insulting to its feelings and re-
dressed itself in that summary a la Bristol manner peculiar to
itself." And claimed that the work of demolition was completed
in a deliberate "workmanlike and substantial manner" by some
forty or fifty ruffians, "in the admiring presence of some ten or
twelve thousand spectators, and of an unresisting magistracy,
supported by a strong military and constabulary force . . .".

The writer asked: "Is it proper or just for a magistracy, in
any case, and more especially in the present, where it is supported by a strong military and constabulary force, to witness,
without making every resistance in its power, the unlawful
destruction of private property by a lawless mob? A question

not to be asked. Fears were at one time entertained for the safety of Surgeons' Hall, and had these been well-grounded, the great principal of magisterial humanity must have been put to a severe trial."

He listed the following four points as results of 'humanity':

1. The mob now had a precedent, of which it would be rather difficult to afterwards deprive them.

2. The rioters, when brought to trial, would plead their actions were lawful because these had been carried out without resistance of the Magistrates and supporting troops and police.

3. Disrupting the study of anatomy in Aberdeen and "causing the sons of townsmen, students in anatomy, to be sent to schools in other places, at great additional expense to their parents".

4. The respectable part of the community would have to foot the bill, in the shape of an additional burgh tax, or of diminution of the city's Common Good Fund, "to pay for this frolic of the mob and Magistracy".

Three men who had been arrested were dealt with at the Circuit Court at Aberdeen on April 24, 1832, on charges arising out of the incident. They were a flesher, Alexander Murray, of West North Street, Aberdeen, a blacksmith called George Sharpe, of Schoolhill, Aberdeen, and Alexander Allan, a private in the Fusilier Guards. They were charged with mobbing and rioting, wilful fire-raising and assault. The indictment alleged they were "part of a mob of disorderly and evil disposed persons".

The Advocate-Depute remarked on the extenuating circumstances which enabled him to accept a modified plea of mobbing and rioting, and to depart from the capital charge of wilful fire-raising. They also pleaded not guilty to assaulting Dr Moir and pursuing and assaulting the student Polson, and this charge was also dropped.

The accused had all been of good character, they were not the ringleaders, and Sharpe told the court he had "merely gone to the spot to examine among the human remains lying there, whether he could discover the body of his grandmother, who had been interred a few weeks previously". Lord Moncrieff said that the charges against them went to the violation of all law and decency. If they had been incited by the foolish delusion that the very respectable gentlemen who possessed the building, or any other engaged in the pursuit, was capable of wilful murder for the purpose of science, "this was a feeling unworthy of every well educated and well disposed Scotsman". They were each jailed for one year.

The May edition of the *Aberdeen Magazine* thundered at the handling of the "case of Allan and others". It claimed that the citizens were "enjoying in anticipation the rather ridiculous figure" the authorities would cut when their part which they had acted in the affair should be "gravely detailed" in court. But . . . "These expectations were in a great measure disappointed by one of those extra-judicial bargains which we are accustomed to see driven across the table by the counsel for the parties; that is to say, the Advocate-Depute rather than put himself and the court to the trouble of going into an investigation of the case, consented to accept a partial plea of guilty, and to depart from the bulk of the charges contained in the indictment. . . ."

And finally . . . "On a review of the whole circumstances attending this affair, from its origin to its issue, we fear that it cannot be regarded as any way creditable either to our municipal police or to the general administration of our criminal jurisprudence."

Lost Ground

—

The Burning of the 'Burkin' Hoose' was a disaster for Andrew Moir. The gentle and cultured anatomist became the target of unenviable notoriety in Aberdeen and anyone who associated with him was threatened and bullied. Ruffians hovered around his house in the Guestrow and callers were liable to be pelted with rotten vegetables or dead hens. A lantern which hung under the porch was torn down one night and kicked like a football by a crowd of youths along the cobbled street. On another occasion two doctors lost nothing more than their tiled hats.

Moir and his backers were rightly furious with the authorities over the destruction of the anatomical theatre, asserting they could have prevented the outrage. They claimed damages from the town and eventually received £235 as compensation.

After the fire, Moir looked around for suitable accommodation to continue with his classes and he set up temporary lecture and dissecting rooms in The Vennel, an 'ugly nook' which ran from the old loch and Drum's Lane to the Gallowgate. By November 1834 he was lecturing in larger rooms in Flourmill Lane and had regained most of his lost ground. In the Aberdeen *Medical Magazine* of January 1835 his introductory lecture for the winter session is reported and welcomed: "We were happy to observe, from the crowded state of the lecture room, that Mr Moir had regained the confidence of the students, which we knew he had lost by the destruction of his theatre some years ago. The distinct manner in which the lecture was delivered, and the quiet attention of the audience throughout, will account for the fullness of our report."

His popularity steadily grew, except in academic circles. But at the Medical Society's dinner in December 1834, his health was proposed and honoured twice, a rare tribute. The Chairman, Mr Cromar, described the anatomist as one who "had done more for the Medical School of Aberdeen, through good report, and bad report, than anyone connected with it". In reply Moir said he felt "confident that they would effect something to raise it to a state in which it never previously had been", and he stated that he was always as ready as ever to do "what little he could do, and always more ready to act than speak".

With the birth of the Anatomy Act in 1832, Moir was left in peace. But popular feeling against dissection remained unchanged and in Aberdeen unclaimed bodies were buried by subscription, while as late as 1835 a horse-drawn hearse clip-clopped down George Street, followed by a crowd shouting: "Stop it—it's for the Burkin' Hoose!" A bid was made to stop the horses, but the driver lashed out with his whip and made his escape.

Moir and Dr Pirrie, the lecturer in anatomy at the Marischal College, both reported a shortage of bodies, but by 1835 the supply proved adequate. Moir later stated that most of the 'subjects' were obtained from the House of Refuge, a few from the Infirmary 'when the matron pleased', and some were brought from London. The doctor complained that kirk sessions prevented bodies of vagrants from reaching his dissection tables, and stated that ratepayers would be less inimical if they were given the power to decide.

In 1818 the Marischal and King's Colleges combined to make the Joint Medical School, but the scheme was abandoned twenty-one years later, when a Chair of Anatomy was founded in Marischal College. Because of hostility and jealousy towards him, Moir was not given the post. But in the same year, 1839, he was appointed lecturer in anatomy at a medical school formed by King's College in a house in Kingsland Place, Old Aberdeen.

In the same year Andrew Moir married a young Aberdeen girl, Agnes Fraser, whom he had courted from two thousand miles away. Agnes and he had been sweethearts in Aberdeen, but she went to Toronto with a married sister and took a situation as a companion or governess in the family of the Chief Justice. Love-struck Andrew begged her to return. In a letter to Agnes he wrote tenderly: "The promise I made to you I hold most sacred—to fulfil it I would wander the world over. I wished to extract no corresponding promise for you, because I did not wish to bind you to anything which you might afterwards conceive to be against your interest. . . ." And: "God forbid that ever I should cause you a moment's uneasiness. I have, by the aid of the Almighty, borne many trials, losses and afflictions, I hope with patient resignation, and many more I still look to bear."

They became secretly engaged, and, although Agnes received two proposals of marriage in Canada, she returned home to her Andrew in 1839. They were married at Stoniton, a farmhouse in a suburban village, long demolished, which stood on the site of the present Carden Place, Aberdeen. Their wedding reception was held in Thornton's Close in the Guestrow.

At long last, it seemed as if Dr Moir would find the security and financial ease which had for so long passed him. He had attained a high position in a field in which he was the master; he was happily married and his wife was expecting their second child.

But tragedy struck. He contracted typhoid fever from a patient and died on February 6, 1844, at the early age of 38. Three days after his death a boy was born to his wife. Andrew Moir was buried in St Nicholas Churchyard, the scene of several of his body-snatching triumphs. His table-topped tombstone, near the Schoolhill gate, is also the grave of his wife, who died in September 1876, and their first-born son, Alexander, who was 6 when he died. Andrew, the son he never saw, became a Fellow of Christ's College, Cambridge. He died in May 1870, aged 26, and is buried at Pau, in the Basses Pyrenees region of France.

His family faced utter destitution; but his friends in Aberdeen contributed to a fund for his widow and dependants, which included his aged mother. Later the Government stepped in with a pension for his young widow.

The destruction of his anatomical theatre made Moir bitter near the end. But the incident, coupled with the Edinburgh and London 'Burking' murders, focused attention on the problems facing the anatomists, served a purpose.

A porter was blamed for burying the portions of human bodies at the back door of the Aberdeen Burkin' Hoose, although it does seem incredible that Moir, knowing well the mood of the populace towards his theatre, allowed such a state of affairs to arise a month after his opening lecture. The strong smell that upset the folk of St Andrew Street no doubt came from chemicals, and not putrefying bodies. Perhaps it was no coincidence that the young men who investigated the antics of the curious dog worked in the knackery in nearby Tannery Street. To 'plant' pieces of slaughtered cattle on the site would have been possible. The rest could well have been left to the vivid imagination of the neighbourhood.

Moir would have certainly supervised the destruction of dissected bodies, although he probably would not have gone to the lengths of some anatomists who kept vultures for the purpose.

The obloquy of his resurrecting days lingered long after his death. The town council were demolishing buildings near the site of the anatomist's house in the Guestrow in 1887, when workmen uncovered a collection of bones. The doctor was held responsible again, until it was solemnly pronounced that the bones were animal and not human. Perhaps an earlier attempt had been made to blacken the surgeon's character by burying the bones near his surgery?

In April 1828, the anatomists made a determined attempt to get the Government to remove the barriers which prevented easy access to 'subjects'. Petitions complaining of the difficulty of procuring bodies were presented by Edinburgh and Aberdeen and lecturers from other British universities and medical schools. The Aberdeen plea was made by Alexander Cromar, President of the Medico-Chirurgical Society.

So began a full-scale Government inquiry, headed by Henry Warburton, into the running of all schools of anatomy. In March 1829, while the Edinburgh committee investigating the activities of Dr Knox, published its report, Warburton, supported by Sir William Rae, Lord Advocate for Scotland, introduced a bill to legislate the recommendations of the Select Committee. Warburton proposed that bodies of men and women who died in hospitals and poor houses and were not claimed within seventy-two hours were to be sold for dissection. He also wanted it made an offence to move a body without a licence and to carry on anatomy in an unlicensed building. Grave-robbers faced six months imprisonment for a first offence, two years for a second.

His proposals sparked off a big outcry from both the public and the surgeons, but Warburton managed to squeeze the bill past the Commons in May, only to see it strongly opposed by the House of Lords, and withdrawn. But two years later Mr Warburton, later Sir Henry, met with little opposition when he put forward a modified version of his Bill in the Commons on December 15, 1831. The second reading was on January 29, 1832, and a third followed in May. Shortly afterwards the Lords gave the Anatomy Act their blessing. The age of the body-snatchers was over.

The Dunecht Mystery

The storm had raged for two nights, but by the morning of Thursday, December 1, 1881, the wind had dropped to a low moan. The rain had ceased beating on the window panes of Dunecht House and on the black skeletal trees, sodden lawns, shrubbery and swollen lakes which covered the sprawling Aberdeenshire estate.

The grey granite mansion loomed darkly above an estate worker, William Hadden, as he hurried to start work. But as he rounded a corner of the Gothic Chapel, adjoining the great house, he stopped in his tracks.

The iron railings which had enclosed the entrance to the family vault had been torn down. Several inches of mould had been shovelled off and the granite slab leading to the crypt below had been raised and propped up. At first Hadden thought perhaps this had been done by his workmates after he had finished work at five o'clock the previous evening.

But he decided to inform the estate factor, Mr William Yeats in Aberdeen, twelve miles away. By afternoon Mr Yeats, Inspector George Cran, of the Aberdeen County Constabulary and Constable John Robb, the policeman from Echt, had arrived at the mansion, and were standing at the top of the flight of stairs which dropped into the dark crypt below.

The Dunecht Vault had room for sixty-four bodies on its shelves; but it contained only one; that of Alexander William Lindsay, the 25th Earl of Crawford and Balcarres, who had died in Florence the year before. Because the family vault below

Wigan Parish Church had been closed for twenty-five years, it was agreed he should be interred at Dunecht. It seemed as if the Earl was never meant to reach Aberdeenshire. His body was embalmed by the Italians, and put in three coffins; the inner was made of Italian wood, encased with a leaden shell, and the outer was made of highly-polished oak and mounted with chased silver. The coffins survived a rugged journey over the Alps; and were lashed to the deck of a steamer in a Channel storm. And the hearse which transported the body from Aberdeen was snowbound for several days on the return journey.

Three days later the Episcopal Bishop of Aberdeen consecrated the new vault and eight men manhandled the huge coffin, weighing ten hundredweights, into a niche in the wall.

Now, on that cold December afternoon in 1881, it was believed that no other human had gone near the place since the interment. Inspector Cran, with a lighted candle in his hand, descended the stairway, and moments later shouted to P.C. Robb and Mr Yeats to follow him. In the flickering candlelight they could see that the coffins had been dumped on the floor separately. Each had been opened and the body of the late Earl stolen. The body-snatcher or body-snatchers had carefully unscrewed the lids of the two wooden coffins, but had sawed open the leaden shell from corner to corner, envelope fashion, and then turned back the four corners.

After the police had recovered from their initial shock they discovered that Yeats had been told of the strange theft two months before! The information was contained in an anonymous letter: "Sir, The remains of the late Earl of Crawford are not beneath the chapel at Dunecht as you believe, but were recovered hence last Spring, and the smell of decaying flowers ascending from the vault since that time will, on investigation be found to proceed from another cause than flowers. Signed NABOB."

The letter had been sent to Mr Yeats in his office in King

Street, Aberdeen, but he decided it was nothing more than a contemptible hoax, although he had the good sense to preserve it. It was then that Inspector Cran learned from Yeats that in May or June 1881, a worker had complained to him of a strong smell like Cypress was wafting up from the vault. Decaying flowers, which had decorated the coffin, were blamed. Instead of raising the slab and investigating the smell, the area inside the railings was covered with mould and sown with grass.

The 'Dunecht Mystery' soon became an international talking point in the months ahead, and in Britain it stirred memories of an older generation who remembered the fear and hatred caused by the body-snatchers.

But the Earl's body had obviously not been stolen for sale to an anatomist. Whoever had taken the corpse hoped to gain financially from the theft. Only a few years before the body of a New York millionaire merchant, Mr T. A. Stewart, had disappeared from his coffin and the thieves demanded a 25,000 dollars ransom. The body was never found.

In 1876 a gang of American counterfeiters plotted to steal the body of President Abraham Lincoln from his tomb. Their aim was to 'kidnap' Lincoln in exchange for a prisoner, master engraver Ben Boyd. But the gang, led by 'Big Jim' Kinealy, was surprised by detectives after lifting the wooden coffin half out of the sarcophagus.

The would-be body-snatchers escaped in the darkness but were arrested in Chicago shortly afterwards. Body-snatching was not a crime in the statute books of Illinois, but the criminals were each jailed for one year for violating the tomb. Great care was taken to safeguard Lincoln's remains and in 1901 his coffin was embedded in steel and concrete six feet beneath the floor of the tomb.

There were even fears at President Garfield's funeral that his body would be stolen for gain. And, during the Dunecht case, there was a similar outrage in Argentina when body-snatchers demanded two million dollars from the family after they had stolen the body of their mother.

The Scottish police reasoned that when the Earl's family took no action on receiving the anonymous letter, someone had returned to desecrate the crypt so that the theft would be discovered.

Queen Victoria sent an 'expression of sympathy' to the new Peer and his family; and the Aberdeen *Evening Express* commented on the theft: "Body-lifting, though common enough in this as in other districts some fifty years ago, is a crime now almost unknown; and the horror raised by this sacrilegious act is, if anything, deepened by the skill, patience, and masterly villainy that seem to have been brought to bear in its conception and execution."

North-east Scotland was rife with wild rumours and theories as to why the Earl's body had been stolen. As more than one hundred policemen and estate workers carried out the first searches of the seventy-acre estate and surrounding countryside, the first theory was that the Earl had never been put in the coffin in the first place. It had been stolen in Florence with a view to finding out the secrets of embalming. But witnesses had sworn to seeing the body placed in the coffins. Marks in the sawdust, which had been used as packing in the coffins, were made by the corpse when it was pulled out. The sawdust, in fact, was the cause of the 'peculiar' smell in the vault. Other theories which came to the surface: that the outrage had been carried out for revenge; that the Crawford family themselves were responsible to give them an excuse to sell the estate. And, glory be, that a newspaper reporter was to blame!

The only real clue the police had at this stage was that someone with an inside knowledge of the estate was to blame. 'Nabob' became the chief suspect when further letters arrived, threatening destruction of the Earl's body unless £6,000 was paid to the letter-writer.

But they also believed that more than one person was responsible; could one man alone be responsible for uprooting the three sturdy coffins from the niche in the wall? Several attempts were made by the family to contact the anonymous letter writer. Adverts appeared in the Aberdeen press pleading: "Nabob. Please communicate at once." Later, acting on the advice of the Government, the family refused to offer a reward for the recovery of the body; instead a £600 reward was offered and a free pardon to any accomplice, other than the perpetrator, for information leading to the arrest of the criminal.

Public interest in the mystery never flagged; there was always something new to keep their curiosity alive. A bloodhound called 'Morgan' provided a diversion when he was brought by his trainer, Mr Spencer, of Wigan, to help in the hunt for the missing corpse.

Morgan, described by the newspapers as the 'famous sleuth hound', had earned his reputation in Blackburn, Lancashire, in March 1876, when it found the remains of a 7-year-old girl, Emily Holland, and helped put a noose round the neck of William Fish, a Blackburn barber.

Mr Spencer boasted of Morgan's exploits in running to earth two burglars: "We started at seven, and by half past eleven the thieves had got three months apiece." He started the Dunecht hunt with the curt command, "Seek, dead", then watched as the animal bounded into the woods. Unfortunately Morgan, described as a sagacious creature, preferred to chase rabbits, even when given the smell of the sawdust that had been pulled from the Earl's coffin. But Mr Spencer did not seem too disheartened with the dog's performance. And the Aberdeen public were obviously impressed too, for on Hogmanay 1881, people paid sixpence admission to the Aberdeen Dog Show in the Woolmanhill Hall to see 'the famous Morgan'. The dog's exploits at Blackburn were not forgotten. In 1888 London police brought in two bloodhounds to hunt Jack the Ripper, on the strength of

Morgan's success twelve years before. But the sleuth hounds never found the multiple killer, and their antics brought ridicule to Scotland Yard, which led to the resignation of Sir Charles Warren, the Commissioner of the Metropolitan Police.

The public, too, had their own theories for solving the Dunecht mystery: methods which ranged from conjuring up supernatural forces through expert mediums, to all kinds of useless information. One 'amateur detective', Mr Peter Castle, an Aberdeen wine merchant, took an almost fanatical interest in the case, and was eventually hired by the new Earl to investigate the mystery.

On one occasion the observant Mr Castle was travelling by train between Aberdeen and Edinburgh when he noticed, 'the suspicious proceedings of two foreign-looking individuals who were in the train, and who had along with them a peculiarly shaped box'. No doubt Mr Castle believed the Earl was in the box, but nothing came of this strange meeting on a train. He had less luck trying to persuade a Professor Coates, who had been lecturing on 'Mesmerism and Phrenology' in Aberdeen, to help solve the mystery of the missing Earl. But a clairvoyant, Donald Christie, claimed the corpse was hidden in St Margaret's Church in the Gallowgate, Aberdeen.

Christie, later dubbed 'The Dunecht Dreamer', was taken under Peter Castle's wing. But his activities were cut short when his behaviour alarmed the sisters at St Margaret's and police were called to warn him off. The Aberdeen public were fast losing their patience with Mr Castle.

In February 1882 the police caused a sensation when they announced they had arrested two men in connection with the theft of the body. They were later named as Thomas Kirkwood, a joiner on the Dunecht Estate, and John Philip, an Aberdeen shoemaker who had formerly been a drill instructor to the Echt Volunteers. It appeared Kirkwood had given himself up in

London when he heard police were looking for him. Philip was suspected of being 'Nabob'; and the police had swooped on the tip-off from a member of the public. His name: Peter Castle. But after only a few days in custody the two men were released. Now the police had lost patience with Castle.

Five months after, the mystery took a new sensational turn when on Tuesday, July 18, 1882, the Earl's body was found wrapped in blankets and buried in a shallow grave, about five hundred yards from his favourite study at Dunecht House. The police had gone to the spot on a tip-off from an Aberdeen game dealer George Machray. On the day they recovered the body they announced the arrest of Charles Soutar, a bearded mole and rat catcher who lived in Aberdeen.

Then three days later detectives travelled to Glasgow to arrest James Collier, a 37-year-old tramway driver who had formerly run the family sawmill at Echt. He was arrested aboard the steamer *Kintyre*, berthed at the Broomielaw, and taken back to Aberdeen.

But although Soutar was kept in custody, Collier was released; he was innocent of any crime. It transpired that shortly after the theft of the body, he had written to the family lawyer, Mr J. A. Alsop, informing him of a meeting he had on a horse-drawn bus from Aberdeen to Dunecht in the spring of 1881, about the time the vault was raided. Collier claimed that a fellow passenger was Soutar, who had regularly worked at Dunecht House and was known to the police. He further claimed he had recently been released from prison after serving a sentence which involved the murder of a gamekeeper by a gang of poachers. But Mr Alsop was suspicious of Collier. He passed his suspicions on to the police, and when the body was found they also arrested Collier.

After further intensive inquiries, Collier was set free, but he never forgave the police and later accused them of 'owlish stupidity' on not acting on his original tip-off.

The Aberdeen police had swooped on Soutar's home at Donald's Court, Schoolhill, after Machray had come to them with a fantastic story he had been given by Soutar while the pair were fishing at Braemar, and later while drinking in a private house in Carmelite Street in Aberdeen. The rat-catcher claimed he had been poaching in the vicinity of Dunecht House when he accidentally witnessed the burial of a body by four masked men. He told Machray they had threatened him with a pistol at his head and that if he told anyone what he had seen he would be 'hunted to death'.

Soutar stuck to his strange tale when he appeared in the dock at the High Court in Edinburgh in October 1882 charged with "violating the sepulchre of the dead".

Several of the sixty-one witnesses cited, including Collier, told the court that Soutar had been seen in the Dunecht area during the period the Earl's body was stolen. They also spoke of conversations he had in Livingstone's Inn, Echt. A farmer, William Lawrie, was invited by the accused to share a drink. And Soutar had opened the conversation about whether he had heard of a body being found in Echt recently. Then he told Lawrie how he stumbled across two men trying to bury a body, but the farmer thought the stranger was telling 'a parcel of lies'.

The trial lasted for two days; Soutar was found guilty and sentenced to five years' penal servitude. The controversy raged for months afterwards. Soutar, on release, insisted he was innocent. But the mystery lingers on. Who helped him in his activities? In his summing-up the Solicitor-General remarked that other persons were involved.

John Philip, who had been at one time a chief suspect, later took the Earl's lawyer, John Alsop, to court for alleged slander in claiming that it was he who had written the 'Nabob' letters, although Soutar was the man responsible. Philip sued for £500, but after preliminary hearings the case was settled out of court.

Three people applied for the reward offered for information

leading to Soutar's capture. They were the Aberdeen game dealer Machray, Philip and Collier. The Earl's advisers cut the reward money to £300, because Soutar was felt not to be the only one implicated in the crime. Collier described their actions as an "expedient of doubtful honesty", particularly when he received not a penny. The reward went to Machray.

The late Earl? He was eventually placed in the family vault at Wigan after the town council gave dispensation for it to be re-opened. The Dowager Lady Crawford erected a granite cross at the place where her husband's body was unearthed. The inscription reads:

> Under this spot the body of Alexander, Earl of Crawford
> (Sacriligeously stolen from the vault under the Dunecht
> Chapel)
> lay hidden during fourteen months.
> He shall give his angels charge over thee
> He that keepeth thee will not slumber

The bumbling amateur sleuth Peter Castle was not given much sleep either; Collier, who later tried his hand at journalism in Glasgow, bitterly hit out at Castle in a pamphlet, claiming that it was his 'meddling' which led to the arrest of Kirkwood and Philip. Which seems fair enough. Castle became a figure of ridicule in Aberdeen, and his effigy was burned on April Fool's Day, 1882. He later became a bankrupt and was forced to quit Scotland for Liverpool.

The century had opened in Aberdeen with graveyard scandals —the raids on local cemeteries by the resurrectionists—and it ended in a bigger scandal, the Nellfield Cemetery affair. But this time the corpses proved of no value; the gold lay in the price of lairs, and so an enterprising official ordered his men to make room for as many corpses as possible. So in the summer of 1899 it was discovered that corpses had been dumped from their coffins into pits dotted around the graveyard, even under the walks and paths. There were eighteen interments in one lair alone inside three months! The *Lancet* recorded at the time that "gruesome discoveries produced much mental disquietude among lairholders, at least one of whom had died from the excitement . . .".

It was a harrowing and horrifying case and when it was all over Aberdonians thankfully reached out to greet the twentieth century.

My First Resurrection

Francis Clerihew studied law in his native Aberdeen during the life and times of the body-snatchers. To supplement his income, he wrote a number of articles and fictional stories for newspapers and magazines. He also joined the medical brethren at Marischal College on their forays into North-east graveyards. He was a regular contributor to the Aberdeen *Monthly Magazine,* which published his strong views on anatomical research, as well as his attacks on the Town Council and the mob following the burning of the 'Burkin' Hoose'.

Because of the general mood of the public towards medical students, Clerihew's articles did not appear under his name. It was not until many years after his death in 1865, at the age of 57, and following a long and distinguished career as an advocate, that the son of an Aberdeen builder was identified as the author.

One of his favourite stories, 'My First Resurrectionist', was obviously based on his own experiences, and was published in the *Aberdeen Magazine* in spring 1831. It is a little known classic and gives an authentic and amusing insight into the activities of the Scottish Resurrectionists.

It was a disagreeable misty night—a thick drizzle fell incessantly—the moon at intervals shone dimly through the grey watery clouds. The gig rolled slowly along the smooth turnpike road. "A cursed unpleasant night," said I, "I'm as wet as ——" "A glorious night, my boy, for a subject," interrupted my companion; "where's the bottle?" "Here!" "What milestone is that?" he cried, as he stopped the gig for a moment. "The 26th!" "All's right! They're to meet us in the glen at the turning of the road;" and the gig drove on.

As we swept round the shoulder of the hill I could faintly perceive three or four men muffled up in cloaks. As we approached them, Sam whistled in a low tone—his whistle was answered, and in an instant they were at the side of the gig. We jumped out, and mingling with our companions, Sam began his interrogatories. "Are they watching?" "Not that we can see, there's no light in the watch-house; I crept round the outside of the kirkyard dyke, and Frank mounted the wall and spied the grave, but the deuce a soul could wee see!" "Any lights in the village?" "None, except an infernal blaze in one of the front windows of the manse, but Peter says its only the minister over his Sunday's night tumbler!" "Why didn't you go and peep in?" "We tried it, but the minister's dog commenced such a yelling that we stopped lest he should alarm the village."

"Confound him!—Maitland, hand us the things from the gig. Come, my boys; mind the bottle, Bill; and, Maitland, take care of the gig"—and we set off, following the course of the burn. We had walked about half-a-mile, when, leaving the banks of the stream, we struck across a rough heathy moor. I now saw the church raising its broad dark mass in the distance, and, when we had advanced a little further, the light in the manse, which Peter profanely supposed to be illuminating the parson's unhallowed orgies. We still proceeded, observing the strictest silence and caution; and having passed one or two houses, halted under the churchyard walls.

Here myself and two of my companions remained for some time, while Sam, accompanied by one of the elder students, went to reconnoitre the premises. They returned in about ten minutes, and, without speaking a single word, Sam took my arm and led me to a large gloomy gateway, where the road from the village entered the churchyard.

"Stand here," he whispered, "you know the whistle? well, keep your long ears on the alert, and make good use of your d——d squinting peepers. Here, take a suck of the bottle, Bill, don't be afraid now,—keep yourself awake—and no false alarm." And so whispering he left me.

As I said, it was a nasty drizzling night; there was not the slightest breath of wind, and such was the silence that I could distinctly hear the solemn tick, tick ticking of the church clock, and the roaring of the swollen burn, whose banks we had left.

Notwithstanding Sam's caution not to be afraid, and pretty good nerves of my own, I confess I was a good deal startled when, a few minutes after my companion had left me, I heard first a noise as of scrambling, and instantly after a heavy hollow sound, as of some weighty body falling on the ground. The same sounds were thrice repeated—my comrades were leaping the churchyard wall, and ticking of the clock, and the roaring of the burn, again fell on my ear, for some time unmingled with other noises. After a while, however, a sound of another description arose; they were digging the grave, and the spade every now and then struck sharply against the small stones in the earth. My ears soon became accustomed to the sounds, and I began to make use of my eyes, and look around me. Right in front of me, at the distance of about 500 yards, stood the white-washed manse, with the light still blazing in its window. On either side of it lay the few dark indistinct huts that composed the kirktown; behind me was the church, apparently a large building, with a thick square tower arising as its west end. Upon my right hand was the moor we had crossed, and upon my left, at some distance, there seemed to be a large sheet of water, whose surface dimly reflected the faint image of the moon, as she struggled forth from the grey clouds, and now and then the image of a bright sparkling star, as it shone out for a moment with a brilliant blaze.

After taking a glance at these things, I kept my eyes chiefly fixed on the village, and the road leading from it to the gateway where I stood, as it was from that quarter that I had been given to understand greatest danger was to be apprehended. I stood in this situation, motionless, for about an hour; not a sound was to be heard but the slow tick of the clock, the sharp click of the spade, and the deep sonorous roar of the burn; nothing to be seen but the objects I have mentioned.

The light in the manse still blazed on, and, as I thought, continued to increase in brilliancy. By my soul, thought I, but the parson is making a most glorious bouse, and of a Sunday night, too, O fie! O fie!

My eye had rested on the light for some time, and when I withdrew it, and directed it towards the road, I conceived I saw something move. Fancying myself mistaken, I rubbed my eyes, and again looked. "Heaven and earth, this is no mistake—it does move," I said to myself. "On, on it comes slowly; what the deuce can it be? I'll wh——" A hand was laid on my shoulder, and some one whispered in my ear, "Bill, do you——" "Hold your tongue," I answered, "and be—— Don't you see it there? Look man, look; it's black—black, you goose; and see it still moves on." "I see it, I see it," said Sam. "What, what wonder is it?" "Hush!" We stood breathless, our eyes watching it. On it came, slowly. I grasped my stick. I felt Sam tremble. I could not see its shape exactly, but it was evidently black; and it still came on. "Shall we wh——" "Be quiet, you ——" "Hush, it speaks," said I. The thing made a low indistinct noise, which, as it came nearer, grew more and more distinct, till it terminated in a low moaning grumph. The thing was a pig! We drew our breath. "Leave me to deal with him," said Sam, "and do you leap the wall at the corner, and take my place; don't make a noise; off with you."

The drizzle had now metamorphosed itself into rain, large heavy drops, and they splashed mournfully on the tombstones as I crept through the kirkyard to the grave. I was cold and wet, my limbs were stiff and cramped, but I leapt into the grave, and handled the spade most manfully. I dug like desperations, till the perspiration ran off my face in torrents. My companions cheered me on, and I soon had the pleasure of hearing my spade strike joyously on the lid of the coffin. "Well done, Bill; come out now; give me the spade, I'll clear the coffin. The lid answers nicely; hand me the ropes." He placed the middle of the rope below the edge of the lid of the coffin; and drawing tightly, found that the hold was good. We then stood on each side of the grave, and getting hold of the ends of the rope, gave a long and strong pull. "Well done, boys, here it starts; another pull, now." An infernal crash succeeded, as the lid broke across the centre. "Well done, that's your sort; all clear. Let go the rope to me again." While he slung the ropes round the subject, there was a pause of a few minutes, "and now haul away, Yo, heave a yo; haul, ye scoundrels."

Slowly we dragged the dead man up; and just as we got him to the surface out flashed the moon, full on his wan, discoloured face. His dull glassy eyes were wide open, and, as I thought, leered knowingly on me; his blue lurid lips were drawn back, and showed his white teeth; his arms hung dangling to the ground, and his head rolled about on his shoulders. In a trice he was stripped of the graveclothes, tied neck and heels, and bundled into the sack. We pitched him over the wall, and two of my comrades set off with him to the gig, while Peter and myself remained to fill up the grave. Our task was scarcely accomplished when we heard the signal whistle. We bolted over the wall in such a hurry as to overturn Sam, who stood waiting us. "Blast ye," said he, "what's the matter with you? come with me here, and hold your noisy clapper-tongues." We followed him in silence, creeping close by the wall, till we came to a dyke which ran at right angles to it. "Raise your heads," said Sam, "and look down upon the road."

The road from the village was just under our noses, and about

half way betwixt the gate and the manse I perceived three men
stealing along. They muttered something to one another, and
drew up across the road. "Hark, now," said Sam, "I heard them
draw their guns upon cock." "There's ane o' the blackguards;
look at him, just at the yett," one of them roared, "Fire on him,
Geordie! Fire! Fire baith barrels, Tam!" They fired; bang—
bang—bang—bang. There was a long deep groan. "My God!"
said Sam, "they've murdered him!" "Murdered whom?"
"Him!" There was another groan, longer, deeper, louder than
before. The fellows retreated a few steps, and paused. There
came a yell, a long, shrill piercing yell,—a fearful yell, of more
than mortal agony. The fellows heard no more; they threw
down their muskets as if they had been vipers, and ran with
the swiftness of lightning. Yell still succeeded yell, each more
piercing than the former. "Run, now, boys," said Sam to us,
and we scoured across the moor, down the burn side, nor did
we stop for an instant until we reached the road. "They've
murdered him," said Sam, 'but run, for if they discover it
they'll be after us." It was in vain that I tried to learn from Sam
whom it was the fellows had murdered. We continued running
for some miles, and at last came up with the gig. "Have you
hidden the subject?" "Yes, over in the turnip field there."
"Come into the gig then, all of ye." I cannot tell how in the
world we contrived—there were six of us—to cram ourselves
into a moderately sized gig, but we did it. "Lend me the reins,
boys," said Sam; 'Where's the whip?" And smack, away we
went.

We pulled up at an inn about ten miles from the churchyard,
and in a few minutes were seated by the side of a roaring fire.
A glorious supper was soon discussed, and whisky punch was
flowing in gallons. Our mirth was outrageous; we sang, laughed,
swore, guffawed, punned and drank deeply. Mine was the sad-
dest brow in the party. I could not get the murder out of my
mind. "I say, Sam, you villain, whom did they murder?" I

asked. "They fired three shots into the poor fellow," answered
he; "a parcel of cowardly scoundrels they are, three of them
daren't face him; but poor fellow; they done for him!"
"Whom?" "THE PIG!" Come, boys, I'll give you a lament for
him. Be quiet, can't you—here goes!" And he struck up a
parody on Moore's melody of, "She is far from the land."

"He is far from the stye where his young porkers lie,
And the red blood is round him flowing."

I can't say I remember very many more of the eventful
occurrences that took place upon the evening of My First
Resurrection.

Epitaph

Today the demand for bodies is as great as ever, and it is being met. But not, of course, from the gallows or the poor house. Voluntary bequests are now serving the entire needs of our medical schools.

Today the strangest-ever battlefront is as silent as the grave. The participants are long dead. But they have left behind their legends, exploits and memorials in the shape of watch-houses, mort safes and table-topped tombstones. It would be a pity if these historical objects were allowed to disappear altogether.

Old graveyards have fallen into decay or been swept away by the bull-dozer. But many are still the same as when Merry Andrew and his cronies, Robert Liston or Dr Andrew Moir and their students went looking for specimens.

Most Scottish authorities realise the importance of the past; Aberdeen Town Council, for instance, are doing a splendid job preserving St Fitticks' Kirkyard, even although this place, like other Scottish burial grounds, has suffered at the hands of modern vandals.

Unique gravestones, such as Greyfriars jigging skeleton, the resting place of James Borthwick of Stowe, a Fellow of the Royal College of Surgeons of Edinburgh, are well worth preserving. And there are other unusual and quaintly-fashioned tombstones worth keeping, even although their owners have never been in a position to agree. They, like the masons who fashioned the stones, are dead and buried. Dead? Most certainly. Buried . . .?

Bibliography

Aberdeen University Review. Vol. 26 (1) November 1938; vol. 27 (1) November 1939.

Act of Privy Council for Delyverie of Dead Bodies to the Colledge of Aberdeen, 1636.

Cole, Hubert. *Things for the Surgeon*. William Heinemann Ltd, 1964.

Comrie, John. *History of Scottish Medicine*, Volume 2. London, 1932.

Grant, David. *Scotch Stories or the Chronicle of Keckleton*. Edinburgh, 1888.

Granville Sharp Pattison, the Argumentative Anatomist by Mr A. L. Goodall, The Scottish Society of the History of Medicine (Report of Proceedings, Session 1958-59).

Henderson, John A. *Annals of Lower Deeside*. Aberdeen, 1892.

Henderson, John A. *History of the Parish of Banchory-Devenick*. Aberdeen, 1890.

History of the London Burkers. London, 1832.

Kinnear, George. *The Fatherland of Burns*. 1910.

Leighton, Alexander. *The Court of the Cacus*. London, 1861.

Lonsdale, Henry. *A Sketch of the Life and Writings of Robert Knox, the Anatomist*. London, 1870.

Ogilvie, Thomas. *Book of St Fittick-Nigg*. 1900.

Old Nigg Parish Church Records—Register of Discipline (1787-1818).

Olden Days in Aberdeen by William Buchanan. Aberdeen, 1870.

Ouseley, Cecil. *The Inhumanists*. London, 1932.

Proceedings of the Society of Antiquaries of Scotland. Series 4, vol. XLVI 1911/12; Series 5, vol. VII, 1920/21.

Riddell, John Scott. *The Records of the Aberdeen Medico-Chirurgical Society (from 1789-1922)*. 1927.

Ritchie, James. *Some Antiquities of Aberdeenshire and its Borders*. Edinburgh, 1927.

Rodger, Ella Hill Burton. *Aberdeen Doctors*. Edinburgh, 1892.

Rorie, David. *The Book of Aberdeen* (published for 107th annual meeting of British Medical Association in Aberdeen). Aberdeen, 1939.

Roughead, William. *Burke and Hare (Notable British Trials)*. William Hodge, Edinburgh and London, 1948.

Scottish Notes and Queries.

Thomson, James. *Recollections of a Speyside Parish*. 1902.

Wyness, Fenton. *Spots from the Leopard: Short stories of Aberdeen and the Northeast*. Impulse Books, Aberdeen, 1971.

Wyness, Fenton. *Royal Valley: The Story of the Aberdeenshire Dee*. Aberdeen, 1968.

NEWSPAPERS, PERIODICALS ETC.

Aberdeen Journal, Aberdeen Magazine, Aberdeen Lancet, Aberdeen Observor, Aberdeen Evening Express (1881-82), *Caledonian Mercury, Scots Magazine*.

ACKNOWLEDGEMENTS

The author would gratefully like to acknowledge the guidance and help of many people, including Dr Ian Porter, Librarian of the Aberdeen Medico-Chirurgical Society, Mr Fenton Wyness, the well-known Aberdeen historian, and the staffs of Aberdeen Public Library and the Scottish Records Office in Edinburgh.